THE WAY IT WAS

Conversations with Iain Tobaidh

a lifetime of stories from Uig, Isle of Lewis and beyond

David Roberts

Published 2023 by the Macdonald Family at 1 Islibhig, Uig, Isle of Lewis, HS2 9HA

Previously published material by David Roberts is reproduced here by kind permission of Uig News, Uig Community Centre, Crowlista, Uig, Isle of Lewis, HS2 9JD

Photography / Images: Macdonald Family 1 Islibhig, Richard Irvine, Dr John C Hay, Pat Macdonald, Comunn Eachdraidh Uig, Kenneth Mackenzie Ltd, Google Maps, The Scotsman, iStock.

Editor: Catriona Nicholson
Front Cover Image: Richard Irvine
Back Cover Image: Alasdair Macdonald
Design: Chris Macdonald

To our dear late father Iain *Tobaidh*,
and our mother Ina.

Since our father's death in 2011, as a family we have spoken of publishing his stories which Dave captured so perfectly over the years in the *Uig News*. These stories have come together thanks to the many *cèilidhs* Dave and our dad shared. Yet, they are a tiny collection of the stories which as children we heard so often and no doubt took for granted.

Our dad was a story-teller, a historian, and someone who could remember the minutest of details that captured your attention, and fed your curiosity. Anyone who visited our home would come to hear his stories, to seek clarity on something, or to recall an event. There was nothing he enjoyed more than reminiscing, while our mum ensured true island hospitality for whoever entered our home.

To Dave, thank you for being our dad's scribe, and thanks to everyone else who has played a part in helping make this book a reality.

In recognition of how these stories have been brought together, and hoping we have captured 'the way it was', proceeds from sales of this book will be donated to *Comunn Eachdraidh Uig* to help its members continue their valuable work in documenting history in Uig.

Thank you from Iain *Tobaidh* and Ina's five boys, Donald, Iain, Alasdair, Chris and George.

CONTENTS

Preface

At one of the wakes the night after Iain *Tobaidh* Macdonald died, in November 2011, the Carloway Minister said a strange thing. He referred to Iain's reputation as a story-teller and that, after his passing, his stories would never be heard again. Fortunately, Iain was a very generous man and not only did he tell his stories to anyone who was willing to listen but he made sure that most of them were recorded for posterity. Many years ago he and I came to an agreement that his stories should be regarded as oral history and published in the *Uig News*. They would be collected, along with all the other historical documents, in the safe keeping of *Comunn Eachdraidh Uig*. His favourite saying, regarding these stories, was "that was the way it was". In fact it has turned out to be the story of Uig, over about eighty years, experienced through the eyes of one man.

When he first visited me, there was no intention of recording anything; he just enjoyed a good conversation, and that often strayed from the present to events in the past that he had knowledge of. What struck me immediately about Iain, was his remarkable ability to recall the minute details of these events; this included the status of the weather and often, clear recollections of specific words spoken at the time. Apparently, this type of memory is called 'flash bulb recall' and is rare. I'd had some experience, in my life before moving to Uig, of people who told a good story but clammed up as soon as a tape recorder appeared. I was also aware that archives are full of manuscripts and recordings that are just waiting for someone to listen to or read them, and then transcribe them in order to publish. Often it is years, or even decades, before anyone does this. I decided that a trusty ball point pen and the back of an old envelope would be just as good as any electronic device, and less intimidating, for recording Iain *Tobaidh's* remembrances.

1

However, I was not going to be able to get him to dictate to me because had he done so, the stories would not have flowed as they did. I hit on the idea of focusing on topics for articles that would be published in the *Uig News* on a monthly basis. My pile of envelopes would grow as we chewed over subjects such as the war, Iain's father's war, croft work, whaling, tweed weaving, beachcombing etc. I was fascinated and totally absorbed by what he told me. To add to my understanding of matters to which Iain referred, I also spoke to other local people and visited the library in Steòrnabhagh. The collected research material and the envelope information would go round and round in my head whilst I was digging drains, turning the soil for planting, cutting grass for hay making or erecting new fencing. As I worked, I would be trying to put the stories and the researched material together into a coherent form, ready for the next *Uig News*. In a similar way, Iain once told me that he never got bored peddling the loom because that only required his legs and eyes, whilst his head was full of his dreams and aspirations. He said that he "built castles in the air and then set about demolishing them".

The stories Iain told me needed to be recorded in written form and then read back to him. It was his job to make sure that what I had written was, in his eyes, 'the way it was'. He was quick to correct me and careful to ensure that there was nothing that would offend. He would say about some comments, "I told you that on the QT, it's not for publishing." As I read he would encourage me with, "that's right", or "that's spot on" and sometimes, "oh no it wasn't like that!" Once he had passed my article as correct, and after we'd made any alterations, it would be submitted for publication. These contributions to the *Uig News* started in 2002 and ended in 2011. We always, rather arrogantly, insisted that there was to be no editing of an article.

At first glance it would appear that I am the author of these stories, but rather like a medium at a séance, I am just the translator and interpreter of information that largely came from Iain himself.

It has been a privilege to have been able to tell the story of the Upper End of Uig (from Eadar Dhà Fhadhail to Breanais) from the mid 1920s to the end of the first decade of 21st Century, as seen and experienced through the eyes of someone whose amazing memory made past events and people come alive: so alive that he often had me believing I had been there myself! Somebody once told me that the articles were not history - they were more about the little everyday things that history books miss out. Well, maybe that is another aspect of history which, if there was more of it, would help us better connect to the past. Now that the era of oral history and the *taigh-cèilidh* has slipped away, Iain's stories are a link to that time.

This book is the result of the desire of Iain's sons to see the articles that he and I wrote together, collected into book form. They have been slightly edited, but are essentially the articles published on a monthly basis in the *Uig News*. They are not chronological but largely cover topics which we thought would be of interest to the readers of the *Uig News*. Not everything in the articles was contributed by Iain because I spoke to other people and made reference to sources held in the *Leabharlannan nan Eilean Siar*. However, all the articles included in this publication were written with the assistance of Iain *Tobaidh* Macdonald.

David Roberts
8 Islibhig

Iain *Tobaidh* - A Short Account of His Life

Iain *Tobaidh* Macdonald was the second child of Angus Macdonald and Katie Ann Macleod. His father came from Geisiadar and his mother from Breanais. He was born in a blackhouse, in Breanais, on 8th July 1925. The ruins can still be seen just south of the turning point before the bridge. At that time half the houses in Islibhig and Breanais were thatched. The building was his Granny Macleod's house which was not actually on a croft. The township had no electricity, no piped water and the gravelled road was potholed. Many years later, in the 1950s, the stones of his granny's house were transported to No.1 Islibhig, to become the new Macdonald home.

Iain had an older sister Agnes, and two younger siblings; a sister Katie Mary and a brother Murdanie. Soon after his birth his mother moved him to No.1 Islibhig and at five years old, very reluctantly, he became a pupil at Islibhig School (which was actually in Breanais). He said he hated every minute there but with such a good memory he should have been an excellent exam-passer. He regarded his schooling as tiresome and irrelevant and yet his handwriting was beautiful and his hand and craft work were held up as examples to which the other pupils should aspire. He found it hard to sit in silence all day and his hand often felt the weight of the strap for talking out of turn. He told me that when he left school at the age of 14 it was like being let out after a long jail sentence!

Iain was generally known as Iain *Tobaidh* or *Tobby*, which borrows from two traditions in Gaelic culture. The way to identify someone is by using patronymics, so Iain was in fact Iain Aonghus, his name followed by his father's name, and this would distinguish him from other Iain Macdonalds. However, there is another way to identify individuals and that is by using a nickname. Iain's father, Angus Macdonald was nicknamed *Tobaidh*. Therefore, Iain *Tobaidh* is an amalgam of patronymics and nickname. (To refer to Iain as just *Tobaidh*, would in fact, be talking about his father).

As soon as he left school Iain got a job labouring for the contractors, Simpson Cooke, helping to build the RAF radar station in Breanais. For this he was paid boys' wages. He also joined the Home Guard. For seven months he worked for the council on the roads. Before he received his call up letter in mid-1943, he had already volunteered for duty, asking for a naval posting, which is what he was granted. He admits that when he left home he was "as green as a cabbage leaf" and victim of quite a bit of leg pulling. After initial training, he was sent to Campbeltown and found himself on a deep-sea tug called *Samsonia*. His ship accompanied four Atlantic convoys to and from Newfoundland, assisting crippled or broken-down ships. At D-day, immediately after the initial landings, the *Samsonia* was sent to tow sections of Mulberry Harbours across the channel, and also towed an old French battleship to create a 'Gooseberry' breakwater there. The tug was also employed towing parts of the Pluto oil supply line. There was another Atlantic convoy to Newfoundland and then on to New York to tow a dry dock to Oran, Algeria. Then it was on to Gibraltar for a refit and then to Glasgow before going down to Falmouth to prepare to sail out to the Far East. However, two atomic bombs were dropped and when Japan surrendered, the crew of *Samsonia* were stood down. Despite the war being over Iain *Tobaidh* was called back from a three week leave to join another deep-sea tug the *Respite*, which was to be delivered to Bermuda. The crew returned on a navy frigate and in October 1946, after two weeks leave, Iain was on his way to Harwich and demobilisation. During his time at sea, he met a few Shetland men who told him about working in South Georgia at the whaling. He survived the war despite the pub in Tilbury, where he had spent the previous night, being blown to bits by a V2 flying bomb.

Iain returned home to help his father and brother on the croft but in his head he was already sailing down to the South Atlantic to Georgia. His departure there was delayed by his brother's two year call up. Eventually the lure of adventure was too much and in 1949 he left home, first to earn a bit of money rock boring at Mullardoch dam in Glen Cannich, and then to Christian Salveson's in Leith. He then signed on for an eighteen month stint in South Georgia.

When he returned home, his father and brother were planning to build a new house at No1, and there was plenty of croft work to do. He was already planning his next trip South and had very little interest in the croft work. However, the death of his younger brother in a freak accident changed everything. It had been assumed by everyone that Murdanie, who enjoyed crofting, would stay at No1, taking an increased role in running things as his parents became older. Now Iain found that not only had he a house to finish but he needed to be weaving tweeds, to pay for the materials. All thoughts of future adventures were quickly dissolving.

Iain Macdonald married Ina Macdonald of Aird Bheag in 1962. Within two years of that happy occasion, his mother died and then in 1965 the first of his five sons was born. Both Iain and Ina were weavers so there was a reasonable income coming in, and there were the cows, sheep and vegetables on the croft. Fortunately for Iain, Ina was keen and able with the animals, because really, his interests lay in the Hattersley loom, the car and his tractor. He was proud of his ability to strip down a Morris 1000 engine with just one spanner and a screwdriver. In 1970 Iain's father died and by then there were three young sons in the house. There were times when the tweeds were slack and

Iain took jobs working for the council on the roads. In early 1976 the fifth and last of their five boys was born. In his well-equipped workshop/garage Iain could, like most crofters in the Upper End, repair and construct crofting equipment using a carefully stored mass of materials he had kept, swapped or found washed up on the seashore. Every village had a dump filled with old equipment in various stages of dismantling, including upturned cars, old tractors, motorbikes and occasionally washing machines. Seen by the uninformed as eyesores, these dumps were not full of rubbish; they were a vital resource!

By the time I met Iain for the first time he was in receipt of an old age pension but he was definitely not retired. There really isn't a retirement age for crofters; there are just jobs that were once routine, but progressively get more and more difficult to carry out. When the pension arrived, Iain would immediately tie in a new tweed and when the breeze was in the right direction the rhythmic clackety sound of the loom would drift up through the village.

In 1996 Iain was taken seriously ill and transported by air ambulance to Glasgow. This was his first flight and he told me that the only view he had was the ceiling of the aircraft a few inches from his nose. It was touch and go as his aortic aneurism swelled almost to bursting point. At the Gartnavel hospital they put in a length of nylon tubing and he was back in business for another 15 years.

Car electronics caused him a lot of frustration in his later years. When he opened the bonnet of the modern cars he owned he couldn't find anything familiar. In the past, if the car didn't start it was the points, the spark plugs or the carburettor. If you ran the battery flat, you could always get out the handle and crank it yourself or bump start it - it was handy living at the top of a hill.

Iain *Tobaidh* made it to 29th November 2011 and it was probably a breakdown of the earlier aortic plumbing that finally got him. He was 86 and was the first of the five babies born in Breanais in 1925, to die. He had survived the U-boats in the Atlantic and Bay of Biscay, he survived the V2 bomb in Tilbury and he came through the scary experience of towing the Phoenix sections of Mulberry harbours across the Channel at D-day. He even survived an imagined but deadly attack by Stuka dive bombers, predicted by a deckhand on the *Samsonia* who had a premonition the night before, and told a nervous Iain, not to bother scrubbing the deck because by the afternoon they'd all be in 'Davy Jones' locker'.

Like so many of his generation, it was his wartime experiences and his time in South Georgia that he most enjoyed recounting, but thankfully he told of so much else – and that is what this book is all about.

Islibhig - with 7 houses (4 permanently inhabited and 3 holiday homes). No. 8 the first house as you enter the village, and No. 1 the last house as you leave towards Breanais.

1962 – Iain & Ina's wedding in Edinburgh

2002 – Iain & Ina's Ruby wedding anniversary in Aird Uig

1948 - Macdonald Family portrait
(L-R) Murdanie, Agnes, Iain and their parents
Katie Ann & Angus (Tobaidh) Macdonald

1948 – Agnes and Katie Mary in
Glasgow during their nursing careers

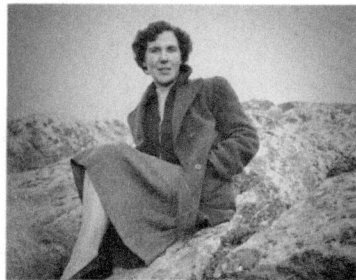

1950s - Katie Mary second
youngest sibling

1954 - Murdanie the youngest sibling

1958 - Katie Ann & Angus (Tobaidh) Macdonald at the new No. 1 Islibhig

Iain with Sally the collie

1950s - George Bethune & Iain taking home the peats

May 2012 - Agnes lifting the peats

1992 - Iain & Ina working on the hay

2017 - Ina & George cutting the grass

Iain and Ina always had time for a good old yarn for those near and far

July 2007 – Iain with his sisters, Agnes and Katie Mary in Islibhig

1975

1979 - George the V at No.3 Islibhig.

In February 1976, George completes Iain & Ina's five-a-side squad.

October 1992 - Iain's wedding

May 2022 - Ina and the boys (L-R): Iain, George, Donald, Chris and Alasdair

November 2011 – Ina and the boys at Iain Tobaidh's funeral

13

Islibhig - a crofting village

2021 – "Opening the gate" in Islibhig still continues

April 2022 – Ina's expert crofting eye and guidance

April 2022 - Ina and George bringing the sheep to the croft for lambing

CHILDHOOD IN UIG IN THE 1930s

Boys and Girls

Over the years I have spoken to a number of people in the Uig district about their pre World War 2 childhood. I thought that the information provided by these people would make for some interesting articles. My general impression is that childhood in Uig before the War, and the childhood of the pupils in Uig School nowadays, have very little in common. Most parents today would admit that it is a struggle to get their children to do any chores around the house – if they do manage it then it is the result of bargaining, bribery or punishment. 70 years ago children on a croft in Uig were part of a team that was keeping the croft and home going. Everyone had their role to play. I was told that "as soon as you were old enough there was a job suited to your age and ability. As you grew older the jobs became more difficult, and more responsible." There were no arguments, the jobs were allocated, and the children carried them out to the best of their ability, without question or complaint. Parents were fairly strict, and authority was never questioned. There were some tasks that were not liked, and sometimes children would mysteriously disappear when these came up!

The girls helped around the house brushing floors, washing up in the stream, baking scones and *aran-coirce* (oatcakes), and feeding animals such as the chickens and the dogs. The cow had to be brought in from the moor for milking, and taken back afterwards. The girls usually took great pleasure from this task. As they grew older, girls would learn to milk the cow but their hands had to be big and strong enough to be able to do this job. They would learn to milk on the most placid and good-tempered cow. Everyone helped on the communal things like peat cutting and lifting, exemplifying

15

how "you were not just a member of the family, but you were also a member of the village".

Boys helped around the croft. In those days almost every bit was cultivated and jobs included picking stones, scaring birds off the seed after sowing, and helping with the horse if your family had one. There were always peats to bring in from nearby banks, in a creel on your back. Both boys and girls were expected to bring pails of drinking water from the well, which could be as far as 200 yards away. There were smaller pails for the younger children, and bigger ones as you grew up. Boys were allowed to plough the ground for the oats with the horse, because (I was told) any "old zigzag furrow" would do. They were not permitted to plough for the potatoes until they could cut a straight furrow, with a perfectly parallel one alongside it. Iain said that "when you could do that you felt like a man – trusted to do a man's work – it was like getting your driving licence. It was something you could boast about at school". From an early age the boys would accompany their fathers or elder brothers on any of the croft jobs. They would help out, and thus learn on the job. It was rare for any instruction to be given, as they were expected to observe, copy and perfect their technique. If a job was not performed properly, you would certainly know all about it. Churning the butter was a job that most tried to avoid. When the churn came out the boys would make themselves scarce. It was a repetitive and arduous job that made their arms ache.

There were very few fences in those days – you took the shortest route possible – often ignoring croft boundaries or tracks altogether. There were only a couple of cars in the Uig district and the track was rutted and full of potholes. A track was sometimes referred to as a road, but it wasn't like today's roads; it was more like a peat track. The road always followed the driest and easiest route for construction, so it was rarely the shortest or most convenient path between two points. So if the terrain, and ground conditions permitted, adults would avoid all bends and hills. However the routes preferred by the children were rarely the most direct – they were designed to take in as many obstacles as possible. Leaping streams and drainage ditches, racing each other to certain landmarks, and jumping off peat banks were very popular pastimes, and made the journey more interesting.

Most townships had a loch nearby, and these sites provided endless hours of amusement. Stone throwing contests or skimming competitions were popular. Causeways to small islets were painstakingly constructed, and children waded across shallow parts of the loch. Model boats were made out of driftwood, with masts and cloth sails. These would be raced across the water. The boys would run round the loch and stand at the point where they predicted their boat would reach. Fishing was another pastime for the boys. They either used the long bamboo poles, usually employed for rock fishing, or home-made otter boards. They towed these on a line as they walked along the shore of a loch. Fishing in the sea was only permitted under supervision until a child was fifteen years old. Even adults had been drowned whilst rock fishing!

Imagination was a large part of children's play in the 1930s. There was very little money for toys. Making do was the order of the day, and this was a good preparation for adult life. The girls were particularly good at this activity. Many of their games were based around the domestic situation. They employed broken pieces of decorated crockery, referred to as *bristeagan*, to represent anything they chose. They constructed bothans out of stones, turfs and straw, often with the help of the boys. They could crawl into these wee houses and play at home-making, and act out family dramas. Like their parents, children were ingenious adapters and alternatives were found when the real thing was not available, or couldn't be afforded. A nice round pebble, with a piece of tweed wrapped around it made a dolly as good as any you could buy! That was until some lucky girl got a real dolly from a sailor brother or uncle returning from a trip with gifts for the family. However, the envy and even jealousy would soon fade as the bought dolly became tatty and fell to bits. The pebble would never age or fade, and a new face could be painted or be re-drawn anytime you chose. Generally children did not feel deprived or put upon because, as I was told: "we were never hungry and always had clothes on our backs. We never had the finer things in life, but if you never had them, you never missed them. There were a lot of things we had that children do not have nowadays. We were never bored and always had masses of friends living in the same village. We didn't know anything different."

The winters were colder than they are today, and the pools and lochs often froze solid. There was always a very cold snap, a time when it was safe to go sliding and skating on the ice.

Schooldays

Almost everyone I spoke to said that their childhood days were happy, although not all enjoyed their time in school. They remembered the 1930s with affection – there were so many children, and people. Every house was open for *cèilidhs*, and dances were held in the street and on the wooden bridges. The blackhouses were cosy and smoky, and pans of cooked potatoes were placed outside doorways so that the children could help themselves when they felt hungry. There was a feeling of closeness, of belonging to the village, with a friendly welcome in every house.

One 'reminiscer' was not so positive about his childhood. Some of it was good but some of it definitely was not. Iain Macdonald remembers his school days as the worst nine years of his life! The tawse ruled the lives of many school children especially the boys. Iain still remembers vividly the 'sensation' of that leather belt.

Mid-august 1930, a crowd of fifteen children boisterously made their way up the hill in Islibhig, pushing and shoving each other, messing about until they reached the *bealach*. John Brown of No.7 Islibhig, who was nearly fourteen and approaching the end of schooling, broke away from the group and grasped the hand of the timid, bare footed, five-year-old Iain who was waiting with his mother at the track above their house. It was Iain's first day at school and he was unsure about it. His older sister Agnes had started school the year earlier and she had told him of the terrible things that would happen to naughty, badly behaved boys. However, that day Iain would only see Agnes when he arrived at school as she was staying at their auntie and grandmother's house at No.7 Breanais helping out. With his hand held firmly by the reassuring older boy, Iain's courage began to return. He enjoyed watching the antics of the other children jumping over drains and off peat banks and chasing each other on the *Geiler*. Slowly but surely, the noisy group made its way down the hill towards the daunting building that stood at the north end of Breanais village.

It was enormous inside the classroom. Iain had never been in a building with such a high ceiling that "almost reached the sky." He could make out 'sticks' hanging from the v-lining, which he later discovered had once been pens thrown up by 'unknown' pupils. Their nibs had stuck firmly into the wood and no one could reach to get them down. Along with the pens there were also ink-stained blobs of paper. Iain felt very small and overwhelmed by it all. There were thirty-one pupils in that room, the younger ones faced one way, and the older ones faced the other. In the early history of the school (1880s) there was a time when there were over sixty pupils in that classroom, taught by one teacher and a pupil monitor. Iain endured his first day with resilience, and nothing unpleasant happened to him. Although the actual events of that day had been mostly forgotten, Iain did recall that it was not what he would have described as enjoyable. What most perplexed Iain was something that he had not been forewarned about: the teacher and all the children spoke to one another in English, a language foreign to him. Even worse, he quickly learnt that if you used Gaelic, your own mother tongue, to communicate you were punished by being hit on the hand.

After that first day things became more familiar, even if they didn't get any better. No one was there to look after him after his first day, and it was up to himself to decide when to leave for school. If he was late, he had to run wildly to catch up with the others. Some days he left on time but always got waylaid en-route. Punctuality was not Iain's strong point; he was never eager to be early. If he arrived after the bell had rung, and without a plausible alibi, he would be punished by a stroke of the tawse on the palm of his hand.

The tawse was a heavy leather strap with two slits along its length. If you pulled your hand away then you got it across the back of your knees and that hurt even more. In those days all the boys wore short trousers until they eventually left school at fourteen. The strap was rarely out of action. First thing in the morning the boys, especially the ones who had not done their homework, or whose memories were poor under duress, would warm their hands on the hot pipes that ran around the classroom walls. The heat in the pipes increased the blood circulation which was supposed to reduce the pain felt when the strips of leather hit your hand. Whether this worked or even how effective this means of punishment truly was, is debatable. It didn't improve Iain's punctuality, reduce his chattering in class or improve his memory for times-tables. In fact, arithmetic was the reason for much of the grief endured by Iain in his nine years of compulsory education.

Most nights there was homework to do which usually consisted of spellings or times tables to learn. This had to be fitted in with the chores and the preferred option out of the two would always be the chores. In the morning it was often difficult to recall what homework had been set. So, after a bowl of porridge and completing the morning chores, it was off to school whatever the weather: sun, gale, deluge or in the mid-winter darkness. First thing in the school morning was the testing of homework. You never knew who would be picked on or when, so you sat in silence and tried to predict who would be next and when your turn would come. All too often you would be called upon to remember the very thing you had not bothered to learn. Other times the answer would mysteriously disappear from your memory at the very moment your name was called. Such occasions were times when the hot pipe preparation would come into its own.

The sound of the bell ringing to mark the end of the morning session always came as a welcome relief. Iain, and most of the Islibhig children, would chase one another up the hill. At home they got a bite to eat, which was never a lot, but was soon consumed. Then there were jobs to be done before returning to school for the afternoon session. Jobs included fetching a pail of water from the well, moving the cow to another part of the croft or bringing in peats or collecting hens' eggs. Racing the others back down the track was the good bit, before returning to the classroom grind Iain did enjoy Geography and History, although the Kings and Queens of England seemed a bit distant from his own experience of life but the rest of school was just horrible. Playtime never came too soon for Iain. What a relief that was because you could speak to each other in Gaelic without fear of punishment. The girls had the area at the top of the playground and played catch against the wall, while the boys had the lower area and played games like shinty and tug of war.

Although Iain was not happy at school, fortunately enough he was happy enough to tell me all about it. Speaking in English and forming the letters of the English alphabet, which were scratched out on pieces of slate, were among the first tasks he was required to master when he started school. The wooden framed slate was kept in a slot in each desk and another thin rod of slate was used as a pencil. Pupils scraped and squealed across the blue-grey surface of the slate to make their marks. If a mistake was made, the offending scratches could be erased by spitting on the slate and rubbing them out with your sleeve. Older pupils used jotters, pencils, and then later ink pens. When the school opened on the 9th of November 1880 there were no books, paper, pencils, pens or even slates until the 21st of February 1881.

Fifty years after the doors of the newly built school in Breanais first opened, Iain was wishing that education had remained involuntary. The original Upper End school had been in Islibhig. It puzzled Iain that every day he had to go to Breanais to attend Islibhig School. Actually, it did not matter to Iain where the school was located, he still was not happy about being forced to spend a disproportionate amount of his time there. It seemed to him that much of what he really needed to learn was being ignored by his teachers.

Once a month a box of books from *Leabhar-lann nan Eilean Siar* would arrive at the school by bus and each pupil was able to choose one to take home with them. These books were different from the boring reading books that were a struggle to get through at reading time in the classroom. Reading time was another of those trials where you nervously had to wait, never knowing when you would be called to read out loud. You could never be sure which part you would be made to read, so there was no way to prepare in advance, it was just a matter of waiting in dread.

All work took place in silence except when you had to read aloud or recite tables. Occasionally, there would be a whisper but you dare not be caught. The double desks were made from wood and had metal frames. Murdo MacKinnon often whispered, demanding answers and looking over the work of Iain's sister Agnes, trying to copy what she had written. On one occasion the teacher happened to see what Murdo was up to but poor Agnes got the strap for allowing him to 'cheat'. For lesser crimes, the punishment was doing lines, which meant copying something out repetitively a hundred times.

Not all the time spent in school was unpleasant. A lady came in to teach the girls sewing and handicrafts while the boys learned to weave baskets, plait raffia and grow things in the school garden. Physical Training usually involved set exercises that were performed on the grass outside the school. The children were also taught the rules to team games like rounders and shinty, the latter being only played by the boys. Drawing was also on the curriculum but singing was confined to those whose voices made a pleasant sound. These mainly belonged to the girls. The boys whose voices were not 'suited' to singing, a group that included Iain, just had to listen. This was okay because, at least, it was not arithmetic!

Events such as the communions, peat cutting, sheep fanking, cattle driving, hay making, potato harvesting, annual sales and even very severe weather came as a welcome relief to Iain. Despite the protestations of the teacher, these activities took priority over school attendance - law, or no law. There were also epidemics of disease that interrupted school attendance. These unscheduled holidays from school were an absolute joy to Iain, unless of course it was his own illness forcing the absence. But even then, it was a toss up whether the illness, or school attendance was worse.

Shoes were an unnecessary extravagance. Almost all children went to school in the summer with bare feet. However, in September letters and postal orders would be sent to J.D. Williams of Manchester. They would be posted on Monday and the order, without fail, would arrive the next Saturday. The demand was for winter footwear, the type required varied; some had tackety boots, others had wellies, and a few would have clogs. These were worn all winter, if necessary and repairs would be carried out by the cobbler who lived at the north end of Cairisiadar. What was left of the footwear would be discarded at the end of April and it was back to bare feet in May. For a few days their unshod feet would be a bit tender and they would occasionally stub a toe on a rock but soon their feet hardened up.

In 1930, when Iain first started school, the infant teacher was Miss Gunn who shared the schoolhouse accommodation with Miss Matheson, the Head Teacher. Three years later Miss Gunn, only in her forties, died unexpectedly during the summer holidays. Iain regarded her as a nice woman and a good teacher. She was replaced by Miss Macleod, who lodged at Iain's own house, No.1 Islibhig. Fancy having your teacher around outside school hours as well! However, it turned out to be a blessing in disguise for whenever the mobile shop came, Miss Macleod would buy bars of McCowan's toffee and share them among the Macdonald children. Perhaps this was to make up for her occasional severity in the classroom! Two or three years later she was to leave her post at the school. Iain Brown, the very one who had held the terrified Iain's hand on the way to his first day at school, had asked her to become his wife and Miss Macleod had agreed to become Mrs. Brown. She was replaced by Miss Macritchie from Carlabhagh, who lodged at No.3 Breanais until she too left in 1943. Throughout Iain's time in Islibhig School, the Head Teacher was Miss Matheson from Mealabost Farm, Steòrnabhagh. She arrived at the school in 1920 and finished in 1948, when she moved to Griomsiadar. For the last few months of the school's existence Mr. Murdo Macleod took over as head teacher. Islibhig School closed its doors for the last time in 1940, and from then until 1965 the children of Breanais and Islibhig were bussed to Mangurstadh School.

If Adolf Hitler and his troops had not been trampling over parts of Eastern Europe in 1939, Iain would have had to do another year in Islibhig School. The Government had planned to raise the school leaving age from fourteen to fifteen. So when Iain left school for the summer holidays on the 8th of July 1939 he fully expected to be returning at the end of August. He was not happy about this. What crime had he committed to be sentenced to another year's hard labour in school? However, with the prospect of war looming, the Government announced a change of plan. The extra year would be postponed for the time being. In August, when all the other children went back to school, fourteen-year-old Iain was perhaps the only person in Britain thankful. He had been reprieved. Free at last.

1935 - Islibhig School, George V Silver Jubilee Celebrations

1931 - Iain starting school

1938 - Iain aged 13

The remains of Islibhig School today

Class of 1938 - Islibhig School

(L-R) Back Row: John MacDonald (Iain Tobaidh)1 Islibhig;
John Macleod 3 Islibhig; JA Macaulay (Nagish) 2 Breanais;
John Murdo Maclean (Iain Mhurchaidh Sheocan) 3 Breanais;
(L-R) Second Row: DJ Macaulay 8 Islibhig; MJ Buchanan (Bodan) 27 Breanais;
J Buchanan (Iagan) 27 Breanais; Murdanie Macdonald 1 Islibhig;
Front Row: Norman Morrison (Dola) 17 Breanais

28

2010 - All born in 1925 - Islibhig School
(L-R): John Murdo MacLean (Iain Mhurchaidh Sheocan) 3 Breanais;
John MacDonald (Iain Tobaidh)1 Islibhig;
Cathie Ann MacLeod (Catrion' Anna) 28 Breanais;
Norman (Dola) Morrison 17 Breanais; John Buchanan (Beudan)11 Breanais;

1929 - Islibhig School pupils

(L-R) *Back Row:*
Effie Maclean (Etta Phoint)1 Breanais; Peggy Morrison (Peideag) 17 Breanais;
John Brown 7 Islibhig; Murdo Maclean (Murchadh Phoint) 1 Breanais;
Neil Buchanan (Niall a Scaff)11 Breanais; Chirsty Bell Maclean (Chirsty Bell Phoint) 1
Breanais; Peggy Ann Buchanan (Be-anna) 11 Breanais;

(L-R)*Middle Row:*
Teacher, Issy Matheson; Kenneth Maclean (Coinneach Phoint) 1 Breanais;
Dolina Morrison (Dollago) 17 Breanais; Joan Morrison (Shondag) 17 Breanais;
Lizzy Brown 7 Islibhig; Kate Ann Macritchie (Kate Anna na Shibealaig) 15 Breanais; Chirsty
Morrison (Luiedee)17 Breanais; Peggy Ann Maclean (Peigi Anna Phoint) 1 Breanais;
Catherine Macaulay (Neena) 2 Breanais; Barbara Maclean (Barbara Sheocan) 3 Breanais;
Angus Morrison (Mex) 28 Breanais; Teacher, Violet Gunn

(L-R) *Front Row:*
Neil Angus Morrison (Buigealor) 29 Breanais; Murdo Morrison (Murchadh Shonse) 29
Breanais; Murdo Mackinnon (An Corbanach) 18 Breanais; Iain Morrison (Dotair Shonse) 29
Breanais; Agnes Macdonald 1 Islibhig; Peggy Morrison (Peggy Choinnich) 28 Breanais;
Katie Macleod (Katie Mhurchadh na h-Airde) 3 Islibhig; Calum Iain Macaulay, (Raaja) 2
Breanais; Angus Maclean (Aonghas Sheocan) 3 Breanais;
Calum Iain Buchanan (Lornie) 11 Breanais

Two at the very front:
John Angus Macaulay (Nagish) 2 Breanais; Uisden Brown 7 Islibhig

Bully Beef and Highland Toffee

Islibhig has a very special view of *Mealaisbhal* from where it appears as a pointed peak. To most people in Uig it appears flat topped. It is the highest hill in Lewis, being 1883 feet or 574 metres at its summit. The west side is in Islibhig grazings, the north end is in Mangurstadh grazings and the east side is in Eadar Dhà Fhadhail grazings. It is composed, like the rest of the Uig and Harris hills, largely of granite. The distinctive shape of these hills was created by ice during the last Ice Age.

Mealaisbhal from No. 1 Islibhig

I first climbed to the top in 1970, which was 33 years after a 12-year-old, Iain *Tobaidh* scaled it with his father and younger brother. At the highest point they found a cairn composed of stones and empty glass bottles. *Tobaidh*, Iain's father, explained to his sons that for some strange reason visitors enjoyed climbing to the summit and celebrating the achievement by drinking bottles of beer. Then even stranger, they wrote their names on pieces of paper, put these in the empty bottles, and pushed them into the cairn.

When the Macdonald boys got back home their mother had a reward waiting for the intrepid mountaineers. The Co-op mobile shop had been and out of her precious housekeeping money she had bought a tin of bully-beef. What a treat for the whole family. Usually, the meals were pretty boring. They went something like this: salt herring and potatoes on Monday and Tuesday, soup on Wednesdays, salt herring on Thursday, Friday and Saturday, and meat soup on Sunday. Most other meals involved oatmeal. Times were hard in those pre-war days, although nobody starved. The croft provided a lot of the necessities of life. There was little paid work available. It was possible to get a job on the roads, but this was operated on a six months work and six months on the dole, turn and turnabout. The dole for a man with a wife and four children was twenty-four shillings a week (£1.20 in decimal currency). If the unemployment went on for more than six months then you could go onto Transitional Benefit. If you were on benefit, the family would live in fear of a visit from the Public Assistance man, in case he found any reason to reduce the amount they were entitled to receive. An extra chair was regarded as an extravagance!

Bully-beef was not the only treat the Macdonald children received. Every week Grand Uncle Murdo Buchanan walked up from No.26 (Breanais), to collect his pension from the post office in Islibhig. He always stopped off at the Macdonald's for a *cèilidh* and *strupag* (cup of tea) and unfailingly he presented the children with a penny each. This was all the pocket money available to the Macdonald children in those days. Grand Uncle Murdo was a bachelor. In his younger days he had been a fisherman who worked most of his life out of Peterhead and Fraserburgh. The penny was always used in the same way every single week. When the grocery van came, it would be exchanged for a slab of McCowan's Highland Cream Toffee. The bar seemed enormous and was marked out into eight pieces. If you tried really hard you could make it last for two days, thus leaving the next five completely sweetie free. There would be two days of withdrawal symptoms and then three anticipating Uncle Murdo's arrival, and the next visit of the grocery van. Nowadays, I am told the slab of toffee has shrunk in size and is 36 times the price.

Isolation

The opportunities for children to see new faces or new places were few and far between in the 1930s. Excursions beyond the next village were rare and exciting adventures. For much of the year very few strangers made it to the Upper End. There was Cyril Goodge's grocery van which came up once a week and then starting in 1938 the Co-op van also did the rounds. Throughout the year, every two to three weeks a gentleman would appear on his bicycle. On the front of his bike there was a frame to carry a large suitcase. He was a very tall and imposing man who was exceptionally polite, always cheery, and very welcome at every house. The women and children were desperate to see what delights there were shut away in his battered suitcase. When it was eventually opened, out would spill colourful aprons, blouses, skirts, and scarves in a variety of patterns. There were knickers and other undergarments, and even some children's and men's clothes too. It was a different kind of shopping from that undertaken in the town. Kerr Singh never expected you to pay more than you could afford. He would note down what you owed and on his next visit he would accept the balance. Money was scarce then: if you shopped in Steòrnabhagh or gave the bus driver an order you had to pay the lot all at once.

Kerr came over from Steòrnabhagh by bus with his suitcase and bicycle. He stayed overnight in Mangurstadh with Malcolm Morrison at No 8 whose nickname was *Zinc*. Sometimes Kerr's cousin Julip would appear instead but he stayed overnight in Eadar Dhà Fhadhail . They never came together. Kerr was always known as *Iain an t' Sinc* in Uig. He was short sighted and often did not recognise people.

He was eventually sent to Glasgow to have an eye operation where Agnes, Iain *Tobaidh's* older sister, who knew Kerr Singh well from his visits to Islibhig and Breanais, was working as a nurse in the Eye Infirmary in Glasgow. When she saw him on the ward with bandages over his eyes, she greeted him like a long-lost friend. "Hello Iain how are you?" His face lit up with an enormous smile "I'm very well thank you. You must be from Uig!" he exclaimed. After the war Kerr got rid of the bicycle and bought himself a car. He still came over to Uig with clothes to sell. From time to time he returned to India and he happened to be there in 1948 when Mahatma Gandhi was assassinated. When he got back, *Zinc* joked that he was on the run, the suggestion in Uig being: "I hear it was you Iain that shot Gandhi!"

There were other visitors who came selling things from time to time. Bob Newland and his wife came from Orkney with lino, mats, and carpets, and occasionally the Stewarts came over from Bruach Mhàiri for the day to sell an assortment of household stuff. Both families were *Ceàirdinn*. From 1928 onwards there was a daily visit by the postman Angus MacInnes who came from Calanais in a van. Before that the post came by boat from Calanais to Miabhaig every two days or so.

Once a year a lorry would appear in the Upper End with a motley collection of young men from other parts of the parish on board. Often they were dressed in women's clothing or other fancy dress, the horn would be sounded continuously and there was laughter and shouting that could be heard long before they arrived in the village. They would leap off the lorry, and dance about playing the fool and some would chase the girls demanding money. The excuse for this outlandish behaviour was that they were collecting for the Steòrnabhagh Hospital Fund. However, there was obviously another purpose to their visit and this was to take the opportunity to eye up the girls. It was also a chance for the girls to see what the young men from other areas were like.

35

It was not unknown for the visit of the fund-raising lorry to lead eventually to marriage. There were not many other opportunities for young people in different parts of Uig to meet. Why the young men thought that dressing up in women's clothes would attract the girls is anyone's guess, but for some it obviously worked!

Iain told me of an occasion that occurred in 1937 and it exemplifies the degree of isolation experienced by the young people in Islibhig and Breanais at that time. A 12-year-old Iain and his 13-year-old friend Hugh Brown No 7 Islibhig were messing about in *Gil Chleidir* the wee glen just north of Islibhig in which *Cleite Aonghais* is situated. The boys had either finished their chores for the day or, more likely, had just made themselves scarce so that no one could find them. Along came Angus Morrison of Breanais with his cow on a halter. Never having been to Mangurstadh before, the two boys eagerly accepted Angus's invitation to accompany him and his cow. This was to the next village, no more than three miles away, but to the boys it might as well have been on another planet! The cow was 'needing' the bull, and the bull was in Mangurstadh. To be certain of a constant supply of milk, it was important to make sure that one or other of the family cows was in calf. The boys set off on an expedition into unexplored and foreign territory.

Iain knew of Mangurstadh because he had often heard the story of how his grandfather Donald Macleod had stayed behind when in 1875 the rest of the village moved to Dun Càrlabhagh and Mangurstadh became a farm. He also knew that most of the people living in the Mangurstadh had once been residents of Islibhig and Breanais and had moved 26 years before to create a new village, when the farm was broken up. Nevertheless, in all his 12 years there had not been any reason to go there. Iain had only twice been along the road north out of Islibhig and both times it had been on the bus. He had visited the Cairnais sale, and on another occasion his mother had accompanied him on a visit to his uncle in Geisiadar.

Eventually the cow and its attendants arrived at the track that leads down to Mangurstadh sands. They crossed the back of the beach and made their way up to Iain Morrison's house, and the cow was put to the bull immediately. Angus and the boys were invited by Angus's uncle Iain for a *cèilidh* and *strupag* in the house. In due course, after the bull had been observed doing the business, they returned home along the same route they had come with a much better appreciation of the geography of the Upper End of Uig.

Na Ceàrdain

In most parts of Britain, the arrival of the travellers was, and still is, not very welcome. By travellers I mean people who move around the countryside and do not live permanently in houses. However, in the 1930s most people in Uig, and especially the children, looked forward to a visit from *na ceàrdain,* as they were called. The family that came to Uig for long periods in the summer were the Drummonds. They stayed in Bruach Mhairi in the winter but as the days lengthened, they would pile their gear onto a cart, and with the horse up front and a few others behind, would set off for the south west of Lewis. They pitched their tent at various places in Uig. One site was just north of Carisiadar. Another site was half-way up the Glen, close to the largest of the quarries, where on a flattish area there are remains of a hearth. Above this on the slope are the initials JD traced out in stones, indicating James Drummond's ownership of the camping place. Near the Breanais School, close to *Allt a' Gheiler,* a little upstream from where the World War 2 powerhouse now stands, was another of their favoured sites.

The Drummonds arrival in Breanais usually coincided with the school holidays and for the children of the Upper End this was one of the great events of their lives. These temporary residents were exotic visitors who had different ways, spoke a foreign language, and could perform 'magic tricks.' The Drummonds, like all the Highland Travellers spoke Gaelic perfectly well but they communicated amongst themselves in their own exclusive language. It was known as *Beurla-reagaird*, a strange pidgin Gaelic back slang, which no-one in the crofting community could understand.

Once the horses were tethered and the cart unloaded, the large brown canvas ridge tent was erected. Inside they had a 'bogey' stove with a chimney pipe that went through a hole in the tent roof. Then Seamus Drummond set to, repairing the previous year's hearth outside. Soon a peat fire was burning, and a kettle of water was warming in the flames. Peats were easily obtained because crofters had conveniently made stacks by the roadside throughout the district. No-one begrudged them a peat or two; they never took more than a few from any one stack. Close by the fire, Seamus set up a T-shape stake, made of iron which he used as his anvil. In his cart were many numbers of flat sheets of shiny tin, two feet by three feet in size.

As soon as the day's tasks were completed, the children of the two villages would run to *A' Gheiler*. In no time a crowd of them had formed around the tinsmith. He was a big strapping man, a friendly trustworthy giant, who would blether about anything and everything, but it wasn't for the talk they were there. They were eager to see the act of 'magic', which would be performed before their very eyes. He started with a pair of snips and a notched ratchstick for measuring. First, he cut a perfect circle, then a rectangle, and finally a long strip about an inch wide. He took a hammer and gradually transformed the flat rectangular sheet. The village children were transfixed; their eyes following his every move, and every strike of the hammer. On their faces were expressions of amazement and delight. Open-mouthed, they watched the flat sheet of tin curve around the anvil, until it made a perfect cylinder. Like all skilled craftsmen, Seamus made it look so simple but, like a conjurer, there seemed to be something unbelievable about the process. The boys often watched their fathers making and mending, turning scrap parts and driftwood into tools, but this was something different – it was pure magic. Then the next trick would take place. Seamus would plunge an iron into the fire and when it was red hot, would use it to make the join. He dipped the iron into some roset (a type of resin) and then a bar of lead solder suddenly became liquid silver that ran without effort into the joint. Within seconds the ribbon had frozen solid and the cylinder was complete. But that was not the end of the performance. To everyone's amazement the circle that had been cut earlier fitted perfectly into one end. Again, the silver solder flowed, and the pail now had a base. The thin strip was hammered into a circle then soldered onto the base to make a foot that would keep the bottom of the pail clear of the ground. The job was nearly done. A patch was soldered onto the rim on each side, holes punched, and a curved length of fence wire threaded through and bent over to make a handle. The shiny new pail joined the collection of jugs, mugs, variously sized pails, and other utensils Seamus had already completed. Probably the most useful of the tinsmith's creations was the *muga cheard,* a two-pint vessel which became a drinking mug, a scoop, or a jug. Most often it was used for milking the cow.

In no time, these pots, pans, pails, and jugs would appear in the croft houses of the children who had seen the 'magic' of their manufacture. It was Seamus's wife's job to sell the utensils to the crofters. The tinsmith's creations were no works of art but they were well made, utilitarian and cheap and were essential to the crofting way of life. They were exchanged for whatever the crofter's wife could afford. Sometimes it was milk, cheese and eggs, sometimes salt meat, or fish, but rarely was it money – there just wasn't much of that to go round. Sometimes the children would be sent up to the camp with a leaky pot or pail to be repaired. Seamus would apply patches and solder or recommend a new one if the hole could not be repaired. The leaky one could always be used for other jobs such as collecting potatoes, feeding the cattle, or taking out the ashes.

Seamus was also an expert with horses, and always had one or two to trade. He had contacts in Dingwall. He demonstrated the horse's gentle nature by sending his youngest child to walk or crawl between the horse's legs. There was never a problem finding a small child to do this job; Seamus's wife was always kept busy producing more little Drummonds! The horse for its part tolerated the child without any show of discomfort or impatience. It was important to a crofter that a horse should tolerate children because they would be the ones tending it, feeding, and moving it to new pastures. He never sold a bad horse to a crofter.

All too soon for the children, the *tiona-cheàird* had satisfied the crofter's need for his wares, so his job was done. The summer entertainment was over. The tent was taken down, the tools and utensils were packed onto the cart, and the travellers vacated their campsite for another year.

The site was left unused over the war years. *Na Ceàrdain* did come to the Upper End from time to time after the war was over, but their visits had ceased entirely by the early 1950s. In the latter years they came in a van and rather than producing tinware, they were buying *fuichean* which was the wool and tweed waste from the looms. By then many families had a wireless for entertainment and in due course there would be television. However, for a whole generation the visits by the magic tinsmith provided a far more memorable experience than any radio or television programme.

An Taigh-Cèilidh

Although Iain felt that much of what was taught in school was useless to him, he was eventually to find a place where a boy could learn all he needed to know about life. Their version of Wikipedia was to be found at the No.6 Breanais *taigh-cèilidh* where two brothers, Malcolm and John lived. For six nights a week it served as open house to the male population of the Upper End. Incidentally, this building and that of the brothers' father, Iain Buchanan, formed Iain's earliest memory. He could picture the old man sitting on a bench outside the blackhouse. It was 1928, the sun was shining and the *bodach*, in his eighties enjoyed sitting outside when the weather was fine, smoking his pipe. Later when the *bodach* was terminally ill, Iain remembers seeing him propped up in his bed. A few years later Iain, and perhaps a dozen other boys, would spend evenings in that same house, crowded together on a bench listening to vivid stories pouring from the mouths of the older men. There would be laughter and jokes, some of which would remain a mystery to the younger ones in the audience until they were a bit older. There were also tales about characters from the past and general chat about the day's activities. They were just whiling away the evening and the atmosphere was thick with blue tobacco smoke. The older men smoked black twist which was bought from a coil hung behind the counter in the local shop. There were two notches on the shop counter about a foot apart and the twist was cut to this length which approximated to an ounce in weight and cost 9 or 10 pennies. The younger men smoked ready-rolled cigarettes and the boys usually managed to scrape together enough cash to buy a packet of ten Woodbines or Players Weights, costing tuppence ha'penny. They would pass a cigarette around, each getting a puff in turn, and strictly rationing the number smoked in an evening. There was an equivalent house where the women and girls gathered to talk. It was the building now used as a barn, close to the road on croft No. 20 in Breanais. Iain suspected that it was a more genteel affair and was devoid of the tobacco smoke. Women didn't smoke in the Upper End until after the Second World War.

In the 1930s, enough time had elapsed for people to speak about the Great War. Before that the traumas of the war years were too painful a subject to discuss. The older men remembered the arrival of the black-edged telegrams with the words: *The War Office regrets to inform you that your son... was drowned.* The women and children would be wailing with grief. Everyone in the family would be dressed in black. When the Armistice was signed in November 1918 it was greeted with relief rather than a celebration of a 'glorious victory'. Then there was the horrific wrecking of the *Iolaire* in Steòrnabhagh Harbour in the early hours of 1st January 1919 that brought another wave of grief. This time however it precipitated a collective deep depression that pervaded every corner of the parish, and indeed the whole island. It is little wonder that it was over a decade before anyone felt able to hear or tell stories of the war, whether heroic or tragic.

By the time Iain was old enough to attend the *taigh-cèilidh* the Great War was openly discussed. The boys hung on every word of the accounts of sea battles and the descriptions of the dangerous job of searching for and destroying floating mines. They were aware of the constant fear of U-boats experienced by the crew of the merchant ships and the ill-fated attempt to defend Antwerp from the advancing German army in 1914 (see *Further Reading*). They heard gruesome tales of the privations endured in prisoner of war camps, but it was the descriptions of the squalor and horror of the trenches in France that were the most harrowing. The horrendous conditions were made worse by the inhuman discipline some of the sergeant majors dished out. It is no wonder that a few of these brutal men were found dead on the battlefield with bullet wounds in the back.

Then there were the geography lessons. These were so much more vivid and descriptive than anything Iain and his friends had heard in school, although most of the information was restricted to the seaports of the world - Portsmouth, Chatham, Sydney, Vancouver, Port Said, Cape Town, Hong Kong, Singapore, Montevideo, Shanghai, Buenos Aires, Valparaiso and countless others. As each seaport was mentioned there would be enthusiastic and sometimes heated arguments about the merits of the location. Mainly this was about the quality of the hostelries, and the availability of the girls. As the tales unfolded, the descriptions would start to become too racy for the 'younger ears'. A glare or sharp word from one of the *bodach*s would stop the story in full flood. However, there was enough implicit information given for the boys to wonder about and elaborate at a later date. These were the stories that sowed the seeds of adventure and travel in the minds of the Uig boys. As they got older the prospect became even more exciting and enticing as they tried amongst themselves to get to grips with the forbidden nature of the sailors' tales. In school, they studied the world map with great interest, especially the ports where they now knew the most beautiful girls were to be found. Nevertheless, they still had difficulty in recalling the capital cities of the world.

Another subject discussed by the older men that was of great interest to the boys was poaching. In those days, this did not mean the illegal taking of salmon for there was little of that done in the Upper End. The exploits of the young men in those days included a boat, long hikes over moorland, guns and long treks back carrying heavy loads. The quarry was red deer that lived in the North Harris hills. The young men went out in twos; one would be employed to draw the attention of the keeper away from the actual killing ground, while the other did the deed. The poachers stalked their prey, and took them down with a single shot, gralloched them and carried the carcass over their shoulders for many miles. The meat tasted all the better for the effort and the illegality of the activity. It was also a welcome addition to a family's frugal diet.

Not all the talk in the *taigh-cèilidh* was of daring deeds. It was mostly discussion about everything and anything. Probably the favourite subject of conversation was general current affairs gleaned from the newspaper but some of the *bodachs* would tell of the olden days, local history and ghost stories particularly for the youngsters. There was also wise and useful advice provided by the old men to the boys. This was where many of the young men felt they received their real education. It was almost the only place where there was any entertainment. It was the equivalent nowadays of a night in front of the television, a visit to a cinema or a lecture from some great explorer. The boys were taught about history, geography, weather lore, navigation over land and sea, animal husbandry, and so much more.

Despite the *taigh-cèilidh* being a place of entertainment and amusement, it was also the place where tragic events could be mulled over and where some sort of sense was found within all the horror and despair. On 12th March 1932, such an event rocked Breanais to the core. Iain remembers vividly hearing the whispers and then the shocked exclamations from the adults around him. There was talk of the lobster boat *Margaret* having disappeared behind Mealastadh Island. There was wreckage found but no bodies. Iain recalls his mother taking him straight away to Iain Buchanan's house at No.14 where Dorothy was now a widow with a young son and daughter and a third child on the way. Then they went to the Mackinnon's at No.18 Etched on his memory is the sound of the heart-rending sobs of anguish and keening he heard at both houses. Christina Mackinnon, who had already lost a son on the *Iolaire*, had now lost her husband Cain, and son Angus. Her daughters Joan, Dolina and Katie Ann had lost their father and brother. Furthermore, there was a distraught Mary Ann Macaulay at No.19, who had lost her fiancé and remained unwed for the rest of her life. At No.15 Malcolm Macritchie's family were inconsolable at the loss of their son. The tragedy, and the deep emotions expressed that day, had such a profound effect on seven-year-old Iain *Tobaidh* Macdonald, that even after 77 years he had been unable to get them out of his mind.

There were local myths and mysteries also discussed at the *taigh-cèilidh,* such as the location of the cave with the swords, somewhere on the summit of Mealaisbhal, which is notorious for quickly disappearing into a cold, thick fog. One day while gathering sheep, a Breanais man was caught in one of these fogs, which resulted in a complete loss of recognisable landmarks and therefore total disorientation. The only sensible route in these conditions was downwards. This meant negotiating the boulder fields and precipitous cliffs with extreme caution. Suddenly he stumbled and fell. He felt himself falling through the heather and moss into a concealed entrance. There were steep steps going downwards into a chamber. As his eyes gradually became accustomed to the semi-darkness, he saw in the depths of the cave a scatter of metal swords on the floor. Eventually he was able to return to the mountain. His memory and the mist had played a cruel trick on him and search as he might, he never found the entrance to that cave. Another mystery was the peculiar green lights which shone on the sea just west of Mealastadh Island. The lights were often noted by the people of Scarp but they disappeared for ever in 1932, the very day the lobster boat *Margaret* disappeared behind Mealastadh Island.

Mealastadh with Eilean Mealastadh (Mealista Island) to the right.

Off Roading

Every village was gated in those days. In the summer there were quite a few motorists exploring the Uig road to its very end. Iain himself and Norman Macaulay operated a kind of toll system. The boys stationed themselves, one at the north gate and the other at the south. When a car appeared they jumped up to open the gate, and greet the holiday-makers. They were polite enough but they made it obvious that they were expecting some appreciation of their efforts. They were generally rewarded by being tossed a penny or two, and sometimes as much as sixpence. If they were patient, they could even attempt to 'highjack' the tourists on their way back.

In the seventeenth and eighteenth centuries, tolls were paid to the owners of stretches of road, partly for its upkeep. Before the Uig roads were metalled, they were maintained on a similar basis. When I say roads, I mean the dusty tracks in the summer, which became muddy, pot-holed obstacle courses in the winter. They were constructed in the nineteenth century with stone and gravel, designed for nothing heavier than a horse and cart. If you were on foot, the road was best avoided, particularly as a shorter more direct route could be found across the moor. However, those with a bicycle, motorbike or more rarely a motorcar were forced to use the road. The council employed a permanent road repairer who was responsible for a particular section. He was assisted by temporary workers who were employed for six months at a time. The section from Mealastadh to the top of the Red River brae was the responsibility of Donald Morrison of No.12 Mangurstadh. Beyond that to the south end of the Glen, including Cradhlastadh and An Aird was the responsibility of Malcolm Matheson No.6 Eadar Dhà Fhadhail. Murdo Buchanan of Uigen maintained the road from the Glen to Giosla, and Malcolm Macleod also of Uigen, the stretch to Bearnaraigh road end. All the work was done with a pick and shovel with a lorry bringing gravel out once a month to fill the potholes. Temporary road repairers were paid monthly which made juggling the family finances difficult. However, in an emergency they could get an advance and this would be deducted from their pay packet. Strangely enough, the Glen remained pretty much free of potholes whatever the weather or traffic. Of course, during the war, the heavy military vehicles caused considerable damage to the surface of the roads which provided plenty of work for the repair teams. When in 1949 the tarmac was applied, all these men were laid off!

Nowadays, many parts of the much-improved Uig roads are lit at night, and outside lights on many houses also help with illumination. But in the 1920s, there was no electricity inside or outside the house. Half the homes in Islibhig and Breanais were single storey, thatched dwellings often referred to as blackhouses. A few of these still had fires on the floor, and no gable ends or chimneys. To go outside on a moonless night, you needed a storm lantern to light your way, or if that wasn't available a lit peat from the fire would have to do. I was once given a fascinating description of a rather frightening childhood experience. It started with a child sitting on the clay floor of a blackhouse with a fog of smoke obscuring much of the view. In fact, to the child, the room seemed to be occupied by the fire and a few pairs of legs. When it was time to leave, the child's mother was given a sickle with a smouldering peat impaled on its tip. It was late, the sky was overcast and coming out from the firelight, through the door, it appeared even blacker than it really was. The little girl held her mother's hand tightly, and the two figures ventured out into the night. The track was rutted and muddy and there was a far more direct route home across the crofts and the common grazing. It was no more than a quarter of a mile to their house but for the child it was a journey into a dark unknown territory.

A breeze was blowing, and her mother manoeuvred the peat so that the smouldering side was in the wind. Immediately it glowed brightly and then it burst into flames. All around them the ground was fully illuminated although ahead of them there were a few dark pools of shadow obscuring something. The little girl stepped gingerly forward pulled by her mother who was striding over the uneven ground. As quickly as it had flared up the peat glow subsided, and all was darkness again. The dark patches remained in her mind. She was fearful that she would fall headlong into one of these hollows. Her short legs meant that she almost had to run to keep up the pace. She tripped and nearly fell but her mother pulled on her arm and swung her around. She just managed to regain her footing as the peat flared up again. It was inches from her face, and she felt the heat on her cheek. She was terrified! Would she be set on fire, or would she fall into a bottomless pit? On and on they went; many times the girl stumbled but each time her mother pulled her up by the arm. There were bright flashes of flame from the peat followed by the velvet darkness. Often the fiery peat came too close for comfort! To the child it seemed an eternity. Would this nightmare ever end? Would she survive the ordeal? Then they were home and in the comfort of their own kitchen. So traumatic had been the experience that the horrors of that night are still vividly remembered nearly 80 years later.

The Bridge over Abhainn Bhreanais

Even though the *taigh-cèilidh* in Breanais provided the adults and sometimes the children with entertainment between the wars, especially in the long winter evenings, it was not the place for the age group that nowadays we refer to as teenagers. The gravel road that wound its way through the village was the preserve of the younger children but the bridge that spanned *Abhain Bhreanais* was for the exclusive use of the youth of Breanais and Islibhig. They made their own entertainment which consisted almost entirely of hanging around the wooden structure. It was in fact a very attractive spot.

Just below the bridge, situated on the north bank of the river are the remains of the village mill. The walls are still standing, but the grinding stones were removed many years ago, and resided in Shepton Mallet in Somerset for years before being returned to their rightful parish. They are now to be seen outside the museum at the Uig Community Centre. The river is very picturesque at the bridge with a waterfall that waxes and wanes in its flow depending on the weather in the previous hours. Rain falling on the southern flank of *Mealaisbhal* and on the west flanks of *Cracabhal* and *Laibheal* eventually swells the Breanais river. At the bridge, it tumbles and sometimes boils over the rocks through the narrow gorge which at this point separates Breanais into north and south parts. On either side of the river are stone walls which were built to support the wooden planks that formed the roadway for the bridge. Each side had a wooden balustrade especially designed to lean on or precariously and daringly to sit on. If you were male and particularly wanted to impress, the balustrade could be walked along like a tightrope. This proved your excellent sense of balance, and your courage too. It could perhaps be compared to the challenge of balancing on the Mistress

Stone on the cliffs of Hiort, on a much smaller scale. There was always the chance that you might fall. One way was the wooden decking, but the other was a twenty-foot drop onto jagged and very unforgiving rocks. However, such feats of bravery were rare, mainly it was chatting, joking, laughing, and dancing that took place at this most desirable spot.

A very young Iain and his sister Agnes, often stayed in the house situated closest to the bridge on the northeast side. This was their Granny's house, where they were both born. It was a blackhouse but had a stone chimney stack and a fireplace. In the evening, the sounds of laughter and music often drifted through the open doorway. To Iain and his sister, it seemed to be an invitation, so they would quietly creep out and sit on the low wall which ran up to the bridge, marvelling at the show. On the bridge and perched on the walls were about twenty or so young people, both girls and boys, all from Breanais and Islibhig. This was the meeting place for the youth and young adults, all single, who preferred their own mixed sex company to the segregated activity of their elders whose formal socialising was confined to the men's and women's *taigh-cèilidh*s.

The bridge gatherings were held as frequently as possible. They took place all year round, especially in the 'black months' of winter and spring. It could be a few times a week if the weather was kind to them. Mostly they just chatted, giggled, and messed about but if one of the young village musicians came then instantly the mood would change. There were a couple of very accomplished melodeon players in Breanais. Malcolm Macritchie was the best but his brother Murdanie was also very good. They mostly played the popular stuff of the time such as eightsome and scotch reels. The dancing took place on the boards of the bridge which made a much better surface than the rutted and potholed road. Those not actually dancing clapped their hands and stamped their feet on the resonant wooden planks in time to the music and the rhythm of the dance steps. The atmosphere was electric. The dancers were energetic and often very boisterous, spinning and whirling each other around as madly as the space allowed. There was much enthusiastic whooping as the tempo of the music changed. This was the *danns a'rathaid* remembered fondly today, by a tiny few in the parish.

When there was no music or the players needed a rest, the assembled company fell to blethering and joshing. The boys would brag and show off or tease the girls and in turn the girls would flirt with the boys; occasionally there was a stolen kiss, and everyone enjoyed the fun. The gathering and the dances were a good opportunity for the young people to let off steam and allow relationships to develop. "The dance music acted as a catalyst" Mairead Mackenzie recalled in Calum Ferguson's splendid book *Children of the Blackhouse*. She went on to say that "music stirred something deep inside; both girls and boys were equally attracted to the rhythm of the tune....one would say that the sound of the melodeon was a kind of mating call". Those were the words of a young woman who experienced the *danns a'rathaid*.

The youngsters in the village, like Iain, were entranced as they sat and watched the proceedings, impatient to grow up so that they too could join in. This was not to be however, for when Iain was only seven years old a disastrous event brought an abrupt end to the jollifications on the bridge. Malcolm Macritchie, the brilliant melodeon player was one of those tragically drowned at the back of Mealastadh Island, along with the rest of the crew of the lobster fishing boat *Margaret*. It was many years before anyone in Islibhig or Breanais felt like reconvening the dances on the bridge. The road continued to be the social gathering place for the youth of the villages, but there was no music or dancing. In 1936 they did hold the *danns a'rathaid* again, but it only took place occasionally. The events late in 1939 permanently ended the activities at the bridge but as it happened, in 1941 dances started up again in Breanais. This time, the location was the NAAFI at the RAF camp. By then the wooden bridge had been demolished and replaced by the present concrete and tarmac structure. In 1945 the camp closed, but with the peace came a crucial change to life in the Upper End. Things would never return to the way they were before the War.

Taigh an t-Saltier at No.6 Breanais
near Abhainn Bhreanais (Breanish River)

Taigh Dhómhnall Phadruig at No.7 Breanais
Home to Ceitag Dhomhnaill Phadruig (right)
(Catherine Anne MacLeod), Iain Tobaidh's mother and where
Iain and his older sister Agnes were born.

View today from Abhainn Bhreanais towards
Mealisbhal and Islibhig

Photos courtesy of Comunn Eachdraidh Uig and Google Maps

The Sales at Eadar Dhà Fhadail

In July 2007, Iain *Tobaidh's* older sister Agnes was visiting Islibhig from Calgary in Canada. I took the opportunity to spend an evening with her, talking about her childhood in Islibhig and Breanais in the 1920s and 30s. One event we discussed, about which her brother Iain had talked, was held annually at the southern end of Eadar Dhà Fhadhail. Every September between the wars the majority of Uig residents were drawn to this point on the east bank of the *Abhainn Caslavat* (better known as the Red River). There is a stone walled fank and a flattish patch of ground and this is where the annual animal sale was held. Some people described it as similar to Uig Gala Day, except that at the Eadar Dhà Fhadhail sale you gained money, whereas at the Gala Day you spent it. Another important fact about the autumn sale is that apparently the weather was always good.

Jamie Dobson, whose family had Uig Lodge from 1944 to 1977, told of a strange tale associated with the sales. He remembers a small loch, in a hollow, to the left of the road as you reach the top of the steep slope up from the Red River, going towards Mangurstadh. It became known as the loch that came in the night. Three cows were tethered in the hollow overnight, en route to the sales the next day. In the morning they were found floating, drowned in a loch that had materialised in the night. It remained a loch for over 30 years and then disappeared as mysteriously as it had appeared. The area is now filled with gravel pit tailings.

Very early on the day of the sale, which was always held on a Wednesday, there would be a steady stream of people on the road. Some would be leading a stirk or calf, and others driving sheep that were mainly wedders, tups or cast ewes. Men, women, and children were afoot, although a few of the youngest and oldest went by bus. Vans, cars and even motorbikes were rare in those days. People came from as far away as Einacleit and Aird Bheag, it was the event of the year, a rare opportunity for the widespread Uig community to come together. It was a great social occasion that nobody would want to miss, even those without animals to sell.

The proceedings did not commence until midday so the whole morning was available for everyone to gather. Chaos often ensued down at the fank, with frightened or stubborn animals to be dealt with, often leading to incidents that created entertainment for those who were early on the scene. Crofters would be sweating and cursing, as they tugged, pulled and cajoled their reluctant beasts. The animals would rear and buck with antics sometimes resembling rodeo acts. Occasionally a beast would break out, and had to be chased and cornered with much shouting and bellowing. Eventually all would be safely tethered and penned.

On the flat ground south of the fank three tents were erected. Two were bell tents: one belonged to the Macivers of Eadar Dhà Fhadhail and the other to the Mackenzies. The third was a large ridge tent owned by Angus Macleod who incidentally organised the whole event. Inside the tents were tables groaning with cakes, scones and sandwiches. There were large teapots and bottles of lemonade for the children but not all of them took to the strong vanilla flavour. For those not used to fizzy drinks there was the experience of taking a large first swig that exploded in their mouths and came bursting out through their noses.

The main activity in the ridge tent was the consumption of the contents of as many screw top bottles of beer as a person could afford. There was also something stronger that appeared from under the table. This tent became more popular as the sale proceeded. Payment for animals was cash in hand. No one could say whether there was a licence but the Càrlabhagh policeman, PC Jack, came over on his motorbike and enjoyed a dram and a screw top with the best of them.

The Breanais and Islibhig children were there before midday, mostly arriving on *Sgail* Macaulay's bus. Miss Matheson always gave the older pupils the day off for the sales or, as Agnes observed, "we were given a holiday but we'd have taken it anyway." With great glee, as they passed Mangurstadh School the Islibhig and Breanais children could see the heads of the pupils there, still having to do their schoolwork. Although they were not given the day off, they were released a little earlier than usual. Most of the children at the sale had some money. It had been carefully accumulated and saved for this occasion. It came from various sources; pocket money was unheard of in the Upper End at that time. Some ran a sort of toll system at the village gates. There were also relatives who came home from time to time and often they would give the children a few pence. Saving any money was difficult because it meant foregoing a toffee bar when the weekly mobile shop appeared in the village. Inevitably there were some who arrived at the sale with empty pockets or purses but invariably the ladies (especially Mrs. Maciver) serving cakes and drinks would make sure that such children were not left out.

Iain *Tobaidh* Macdonald first visited the autumn sale in 1935 when he was ten years old. It was a great adventure for him for he had never been that far north before. The first thing that struck him was the smooth concrete surface of the bridge over the Red River; the Breanais bridge just had rough wooden planks. He had travelled in *Sgail's* bus, the fare having been paid by his father. In his pocket he had coins amounting in value to the princely sum of three shillings. He was amazed to see so many people and it was the largest social gathering he had ever attended. The place was packed; there must have been hundreds. There were women blethering nineteen to the dozen, gossiping about their neighbours and catching up on family news. There were very few telephones in those days. Long parted friends and relatives hugged and slapped each other's backs, storytelling, bragging, joking and boasting.

Not everyone was there for the animal sales. There were young men putting the world to rights, often debating heatedly with arguments getting 'hotter' as more and more screw tops were drunk. On the fringes, down on the sands or on the road, were young men and women flirting and posturing, taking this rare opportunity to meet prospective partners. Groups of young girls formed, and after having consumed their fill of cakes and fizzy drinks, linked arms and strolled down onto the sands below Eadar Dhà Fhadhail, joking, giggling and revelling in their freedom from school and domestic chores. Some made their way up the Carnais road to the homes of their relatives. Others went up the Eadar Dhà Fhadhail road to Peter Macritchie's shop to feast their eyes on the rows of sweetie jars and other exciting goods, the like of which they never saw in the Islibhig and Breanais shops. If they still had any money left it was spent on Peter's exotic confectionary. The boys were content to feast on sandwiches and cakes and then squeeze themselves into any gap in the throng of men crowded around the fank walls.

At midday the sale got under way. The auctioneer, Angus Smith (Angus Holm) climbed on top of the wall and steered the proceedings. He was quite a character, with a quick wit and always ready to banter with the audience. Amongst the throng were butchers from Steòrnabhagh and buyers from away. One was Duncan MacCallum from Dingwall but others came from Ullapool, Inverness and Evanton. Crowded around the stone walls were the optimistic owners of the animals, hoping that prices would be good. If the first beasts went for good money to Duncan MacCallum, everyone expected that they would be happy at the end of the day. If not, you would just have to accept it, however bad. The boys enjoyed the entertainment, the bidding, the competition, and the witty comments exchanged, some mildly insulting but always delivered with good humour and generally received in the same spirit. It was all great fun and the boys often joined in with exaggerated bravado, shouting their own contributions, hoping not to be recognised in the crowd. If you watched carefully, it was plain that there was nodding and winking going on between some of the butchers, buyers and a few crofters. This was all part of the game, and there was always some suspicion that conspiracy was afoot.

As the crofters were paid cash in hand, the ridge tent got busier with the sale of beer and whisky and very soon some of the *bodach*s were a bit worse for wear. Their journey home would be a long and stumbling event. Gradually, after all the animals were sold and the auctioneer and buyers had departed in their cars, the assembled inhabitants of Uig bade their farewells and dispersed homewards to the far-flung parts of the parish. Hopefully many were richer, some merrier, and most were pleased to have attended such a sociable and enjoyable occasion.

The next day, when the children returned to school they were dismayed to find that the fun of the previous day had to be converted into words. Written on the blackboard was the task for the day: an essay entitled 'My Day at the Sales.'

The last of these sales took place in 1939. War had been declared but the event still took place because this was the period known as the phoney war when hostilities had not yet commenced. Everyone was rightly apprehensive about the future; memories were drawn to the last great conflict with Germany, and to the young men who never returned home from that one. This was to be the very last of the Uig-wide sales to take place in Eadar Dhà Fhadhail . There were four Breanais lads there, on their first leave after call-up. They had been posted to the *Dunnottar Castle*, an armed merchant cruiser which incidentally had over forty Lewismen in its crew. One of the Breanais boys attending that day did not survive the war. Sadly Neil Buchanan RNR was killed at the invasion of North Africa.

Before the war there were no lorries to transport the sale animals to Steòrnabhagh so Malcolm Buchanan (No.6 Breanais) along with his dog, had the job of walking them all the way. At 'cattle pace' it was a time-consuming journey and at An t-Acha Mór they had to be penned for the night. They did not arrive at the Auction Mart on Einacleit Road until the following afternoon.

Eadar Dhà Fhadhail (Ardroil) fank stone wall on the right the site of the annual sheep sales.

View from top of Abhainn Dearg to Eadar Dhà Fhadhail

Photos courtesy of Google Maps

LIFE IN THE UPPER END
(1940-1970)

Electricity

In March 1954 the poles and the cable arrived that brought the magic juice into the Upper-Enders houses. The magic juice of course being electricity. Not that Breanais had been without electric lighting before 1954 because in 1941 there had been plenty of it if you visited the military buildings. In the houses before the War there would be two or three oil lamps which would sit on a table or be hung on the wall. There was sufficient light for most activities, but it amazes those who experienced it, that they read the newspaper without a problem. Now during an interruption in power supply, they cannot believe how much eye strain it causes. At that time only Kate Macaulay at No.19 could work at night by the bright light, and the warmth, of the first Tilley in Breanais. It was much admired and envied by everyone. At night, light shone from the windows of her home and inside there was the hissing, wheezing, and mumbling of the paraffin powered pressure lamp. When the work on the military buildings started in 1941 everyone was able to afford these lamps. There were three makes of incandescent lamps; the Tilley, the Coleman that had two mantles but a separate pump that made it inconvenient to use, and the Aladdin, which was silent but was prone to unexpected flare-ups. Many people also bought primus stoves, so that when they first got up in the morning it was not just a case of putting some peat on the stove, but also lighting some methylated spirits in the ring under the primus burner. *Tobaidh*, Iain *Tobaidh's* father, was always an impatient man and would often start pumping far too soon. Bright orange flames would shoot upwards and singe his eyebrows. It was not until 1952 that people replaced their 'roarers' with the quiet Calor gas rings for their early morning 'cupan teath'.

(Mind you, out at Hamnaway you could have enjoyed electric lighting as early as 1940. Sammy Newall, of the mill company S.A.Newall and Sons Limited, Steornabhagh, had bought the house and installed a generator).

Unfortunately for Breanais, the electric light disappeared in 1946 when the RAF camp closed and the villagers also lost their local accumulator charging facilities. Instead, they had to go to Mangurstadh radio station for this unofficial service. During the war many people had purchased, and were now addicted to, their wireless. Those who could afford them bought the newly invented dry batteries. But whether it was the accumulator or the dry battery you relied on, there came a time when these went flat. This reminds me of an amusing, if rather poignant story from the wartime period. Just like nowadays, it wasn't always possible to listen to a broadcast without the unexpected, and very irritating interruption of a power cut. Accumulators, just like the mains electricity, can suddenly run out of juice. During an important wartime broadcast the wireless was surrounded by a crowd of eager ears, anxious to hear the news from overseas. In a dark corner, sat an old lady who was a bit hard of hearing. Suddenly there was silence from the wireless, and someone banged his hand on the top to get it back to life, but to no avail. "Oh no. The accumulator has gone down!" was the angry and frustrated chorus. At this point the old lady looked up with a very worried expression on her face and in a rather querulous voice, said "Oh dear. I do hope there weren't any Lewis boys on board!"

In the mid-1940s, a young Frank Fraser Darling was working for the Board of Agriculture and wrote a book about some of his ideas for improving crofting practices. He saw the dawning of a great new age for crofting. There would be fertilizer in bags, and machines to reduce physical effort and improve efficiency, and in case the recently elected Labour Government could not improve the weather as well as everything else, then there would be special facilities to produce hay. At the time, many Highland lochs and valleys were beginning to bustle with activity, as dams were built, pipes laid, and turbines installed. Many *Uigeachs* crossed the Minch to work on these various hydro schemes. The hours were long, but the wages were good. Hydro-electricity was going to be so cheap to produce that, apart from the distribution costs, it would almost be free. However, Mr. Darling realised that if the remoter crofting areas did not make a case for it, then they may miss out entirely. One idea he proposed was that each village built a drying barn that would have racks for wet grass and big fans with heating elements. In a matter of 24-36 hours you could be taking away your winter supply of hay to store in the byre. The cost of running these hay driers was expected to be minimal.

Whatever happened to the drying barns? Well even without them, it was obviously decided by someone that the remotest parts should not be deprived of the 'cheap' electricity. Although for some people, when it did arrive, it turned out to be too expensive to waste on illumination, so they only switched on 'the electric' long enough for it to light the Tilley. In the early 1950s the poles began to gradually creep along the Uig road with the Lower End of the parish getting the first connections in 1952. In 1954 the RAF camp at Aird was completed, and the final poles were erected in Breanais in March of that year.

A single cable ran down to each house and connected to a meter just inside the doorway. It was up to the householders to arrange the internal wiring anyway they chose. The camp at Aird had provided a lot of work and wages so many people were able to buy the appliances to plug in. There were such new-fangled things as single tub washing machines with power wringers, refrigerators, and vacuum cleaners. Those who waited a while before buying were able to make choices based on the bad experiences of those who were too impatient. For instance, if you got a washing machine it was a good idea to go for one with a heater then you didn't have to cope with all the pans on the stove. Another mistake people made was to buy the smallest freezer because it was cheaper, only to find that they could have filled it twice over. The men soon discovered that an electric drill was a very handy machine. In no time at all things had not only become a lot easier, but this electricity stuff had become an essential part of life, and most of the oil lamps had gone over the cliff.

The only complaints I have heard about the coming of the electric concerned the matter of *suiridhe* (courting). Those surreptitious activities that once went on in the darker recesses were no longer possible when rooms were floodlit. Nor was it so easy to creep unseen around the village to make those secret night-time visits!

Iain *Puff* and his uncle who lived in Einacleit were not keen on electricity bills. The old man, in particular, was not keen on wasting money on the electric light. He was in the habit of going to his neighbours, the Mathesons, to watch their television until about 10.30 at night. When he returned he expected a bowl of porridge to be ready for him before he retired for the night. Iain *Puff* would prepare the porridge and then go down to the Matheson's himself to watch the television until about midnight. Anyway, this night the *bodach* came back home and as usual, in order to save money, did not put on the light. He sat down and reached for the tin of treacle, which he enjoyed with his porridge. He scooped out two good spoonfuls into the porridge and ate the lot. When Iain *Puff* got back and put on the light he was appalled at what he saw. There was blood everywhere, and in a glass on the table were the *bodach's* false teeth, also covered in blood. Fearing what else he would find Iain rushed to the old man's bedroom only to find that nothing was amiss. The *bodach* was alive and well, although he was fairly cross at having been woken. When he got back to the kitchen Iain found the tin of treacle on the shelf but on the table was the open tin of red paint that had been used earlier in the day to repaint the telephone box across the road.

Water

Before the new Macdonald house at No.1 Islibhig was built in 1955, all the water used in the old house and on the croft came from the well and had to be fetched in buckets. It wasn't a constant supply either. Many summers had long dry spells and the wells dried up. Fortunately 'Old Faithful', the well across the road from No.8 never ran dry but the 500-yard walk, with heavy buckets, was a real pain.

An improvement included in the grant for new houses was a roof water scheme. This consisted of a 500-gallon tank on the side of the house, into which all the rainwater was diverted. This water could then be piped into the house to the new and exciting flush toilet, and to the sink for washing and cleaning. Drinking water still had to be bucketed from the well and put into a barrel. In 1962 even this changed. Iain Macdonald had been thinking for some years about easing the problem of the buckets. However, thinking was converted to action once Ina, his new bride, had settled in at No.1. He set to and built a tank near the well and fitted a pipe that took the water directly into the kitchen. So only in those long days of summer, when once again drought hit the drinking water supply, did the walk to 'Old Faithful' become necessary.

Even though from 1941 to 1945 there were schemes to supply the military buildings at Mealastadh and Breanais with water, the rest of Breanais and Islibhig were without piped mains water. In 1965, word reached the Upper End that the Lower End was getting mains water. There was a promise of a separate scheme but it was almost forgotten with the seamen's strike causing serious disruption to the country in the early summer of 1966. The local fishing fleet were making serious money running supplies from Kyle of Lochalsh, and Skye to Lewis and Harris. It was not until July that the Prime Minister, Mr. Wilson was able to heave a sigh of relief and the ships started sailing again. At the same time a Northern Irishman called Joseph Reynolds, set up his head office, a caravan, in the small quarry opposite No.8 Islibhig.

The day work started on the Breanais and Islibhig water scheme was the day the first *Loch Seaforth* recommenced the Minch run. Kenny Maclean and Calum Buchanan of Breanais, Donald Morrison of Eadar Dhà Fhadhail and Kenny Macdonald of An Riof were those responsible for the "hashing" and the "Hasher in Chief" was the Irishman. His rallying cry was always "If we can get away with it" and with the luck of the Irish, he did, by and large. To the outside observer, it seemed the whole scheme was done in a slap and dash way. Work commenced at *Loch na Clibhe* where the outlet was built and this was the only part that needed repair, at a later date when it became clogged up. Unlike the scheme in the lower end of the parish this one used plastic pipe and was laid in as straight a line as possible to connect the houses. Each house had a stopcock provided by the council and it was up to the householder to pipe the water into the house. It took best part of a year to complete the job. So, in the summer of 1967 everyone could forget the trips to the well. Iain's appreciation was clear: "What a difference it made! You didn't have to think about water anymore. It just came at the turn of the tap, and as much as you liked. Without mains water we could never have had washing machines and the like".

The old house at No 1 Islibhig, built in late 1800s, originally with a Post Office in the front porch where the letter box is still visible today.

The new house at No. 1 Islibhig, built in 1955 with the loom shed added shortly after.

The Islibhig phone box at No. 3 installed in 1952

No. 1 Islibhig - old and new houses with kitchen extension added in 1985.

Shops

The first shop at the Upper End of Uig was not land based. The goods came by sea in *Ruaraidh Aonghais Oig's* boat from Breascleit. He arrived at *Ramarageo*, Breanais with basic provisions several times a year when the weather was favourable. In Breascleit they regarded him as a bit foolhardy and predicted that on one of his sailing trips he would be drowned. In fact he survived his many trips around *Gallan Head* to Breanais, but was killed on the Pentland Road when he fell off his horse drawn cart and was run over.

There was also a boat from Glasgow that moored at Miabhaig. Someone came round the houses in advance and took orders for supplies. Small boats rowed out to the Glasgow boat to collect the supplies. This was a very popular activity for some in the community because there was a bar on board. The steward often gave some of the *bodach*s free drinks so that he and the crew could enjoy watching their antics as they tried to steer for the landing place. This often turned out to be quite a spectacle with the *bodach*s rowing around in endless drunken circles.

The first shop in Breanais was opened at No.17 in the 1920s by Norman Morrison and was a wooden shed, just north of the present house at No.17 but closer to the road. When Norman left to become a missionary and later a minister, his brother Donald took over. The shop continued until just after the Second World War. John Maclean opened a second shop at No.1 sometime after Norman Morrison. It was close to the house on the north side. He and his wife served in it until it closed about 1960.

It was mostly dry goods that were sold such as tea which came in chests, sugar that came in sacks, jam and marmalade were in clay jars, cheese came in whole round

71

cheeses that were cut with a wire, bacon was in rolls that were sliced on a machine and sweeties came in large glass jars. Other essentials were 'penny tinkers' that were patches for mending holes in saucepans, kettles and pails, bootlaces made of leather that were cut off to length, hay netting, coir rope for tying corn stacks, sheep shears, Ness biscuits and paraffin which was vital for lighting fires before the electricity. At that time the shops were supplied by the buses which brought bulk orders from Steòrnabhagh.

The local shops were used for essentials while other items could be ordered from the bus driver. If you gave him your order and the money, he would get most things for you and deliver them to your gate.

In Islibhig there was a shop built at the north end of the house on No.8. It was a corrugated iron shed with a counter and a door from the shop directly into the house. It was run by Norman *Sgail* Macaulay, who also had a twelve-seater bus which ran into Steòrnabhagh two or three times a week. The shop ceased to operate around 1950.

There was a post office in Islibhig before 1890. The original building, complete with letter-box can still be seen as the porch on the old house at No.1. This is now a henhouse. When the Macaulays left No.1 in 1921, the post office moved to No.3 where it remained until it closed in 2001. In the 1930s a telephone was installed. You had to book an appointment in advance to make a call. Murdo Macleod would make the connection for you and if it was a local call he would time you and charge accordingly. If it was a long-distance call then the charge was calculated at the Steòrnabhagh exchange. Iain *Tobaidh* recalled that to phone his aunt in Dumfries, the call cost 3/6. He would put in his money and press button A. After three minutes the operator would intervene with: "Your time is up caller, finish your conversation now, or do you want to pay for extra time?"

The local exchange was in Timsgerraidh, at No.8. There was not much privacy for phone calls in those days. In the Islibhig post office anyone could be listening and Murdo had to listen because he was timing you. It was also the job of the operator at the local exchange to inform you when your time was up, so they would also be listening! I was told of a time when Iain Macdonald of Miabhaig was making a call and was suspicious that his conversation was being overheard. "You can put that that phone down now" was the accusation. "It isn't up" came the reply from the exchange!

In 1952 the telephone kiosk appeared in Islibhig. One New Year, Ina and Iain got to the kiosk at the back of midnight to make their greetings call. They put in their 3/- and to their delight no one intervened after three minutes, nor after three quarters of an hour but by then they had run out of things to say and reluctantly replaced the receiver. The first family to get a private telephone in Islibhig were the Montgomerys at No.4. They would allow others to use their phone rather than the one at the post office. Once the public kiosk arrived, fewer people used the phone at No.4 except when it was out of order – which was quite often.

A popular way of getting urgent messages to people was by telegram. This would arrive at the post office and someone had to then deliver it in a sealed envelope. During the war the arrival of a telegram was dreaded. All too often it was bad news. Sometimes though, it was asking the bus driver to hold on in Steòrnabhagh until the ferry arrived because a serviceman was due home on leave. The telegrams were delivered by anyone who had a bicycle. This was often Iain *Tobaidh* who earned sixpence to go to Breanais and a shilling to Mangurstadh.

Telegraph poles were erected between Islibhig and Breanais in the 1930s. In 1942 this wire was extended to Mealastadh for military use but in 1948 the poles and wire were removed as far back as Islibhig. Until the early 1970s the poles were a familiar sight but then the cables were put underground. There was a single wire to Islibhig, which often broke in a gale at the *Geodh Sgoilte*.

In 1933 or 1934 Cyril Goodge started a grocery van, which came up to Breanais every Friday. It had fresh bread and a better variety of sweeties than the local shops. In 1938 the Co-op van appeared for the first time. It had cheaper produce and gave a dividend. In the 1950s Lipton's sent a grocery van as far as Breanais. Both these vans stopped in the 1960s. After that Angie Murray had a mobile shop on the run and there was also a van from Tolsta Chaolais.

The grocery vans eventually killed off the small and very basic village shops. However, in the early 1970s, the petrol pump installed by Cyril Goodge was moved from Maibhaig to Timsgerraidh and Neil Macleod (*Niall Cheois*) and his wife Agnes opened a wee shop in an old caravan. In the late 1970s Calum and Mairead Morrison took over the shop and added a portacabin and ran a grocery van. When the post office closed in Timsgerraidh it was moved down to the shop. In 1987 new premises were built, but a declining population, and many customers preferring to do a weekly or fortnightly trip to the supermarkets in Steòrnabhagh meant profits fell to uneconomic levels. In 2004 Calum and Mairead decided to put the shop up for sale. The business was advertised but there was little interest, so with the help of Public Funds the shop became a Community Enterprise.

The Uig Road

Roads are such an important part of our lives nowadays that it is difficult to imagine a time when a sea journey was easier than one on land. It is also a big surprise to hear that fifty years ago few Uig people felt the need to visit Steòrnabhagh at all. I recall my first trip to Uig in 1970 very vividly. I was in a mini-van and was driven at some speed from Steornabhagh to Mangurstadh road end and then back again before the ferry left on its return trip to Kyle of Lochalsh. The Uig road felt as though it had been laid on railway sleepers, and by great design it managed to link up every *cnocan* (hill), each with a blind summit and a turn at the top, always in the opposite direction that I expected. I can safely say that the voyage to Mangurstadh was a lot rougher than the six-and-a-half-hour trip, in a force eight gale, back to the mainland. I am told that in comparison with the road 53 years ago, there was nothing to complain about.

A hundred years earlier Sir James Matheson, the proprietor of the island, planned a complete network of roads. In 1844 there were only 44 miles of road and one horse drawn vehicle on the whole island but by 1883 there were 200 miles of road in Lewis and Harris. He had planned an extension from Mealastadh to Aline, but this was never completed. The Uig road was laid in the 1850s. The purpose was not to provide easier access to places for local people but for the speedier transportation of fish and shellfish. The kelp industry in Uig which had been so profitable for 60 years or so had collapsed but lobsters, mussels, whelks, oysters, cod, and ling were valuable.

The road was constructed by pouring stones onto the track until a hard base was formed and gravel was placed on top to smooth the surface. In places, the road cut across an expanse of peat and it needed a lot of stone before it became firm. In most places the original road still exists beneath the tarmac, and when buses or lorries pass over some sections it is possible to see and feel the movement. The best bit of road was in Glen Bhaltos which was only constructed in the 1930s, when the road was moved down into the Glen.

In the 1920s, Murdo Maciver of Breanais had a motorbike. He worked for the Post Office and was mechanically minded. In the 1930s there were four cars in Uig. The two ministers had cars and one was a Vauxhall. The doctor had a car and so did Norman Mackay, the Public Assistance Officer, who had a Ford 8. There was also the Morris van that brought the mails. Motorbikes were driven by Donald Macaulay, No.19 Breanais who had an O.E.C. and John Morrison of No.20 Breanais had a B.S.A. They were both joiners and had the money and the need to travel to their work. Louis Macdonald of Eadar Dhà Fhadhail also had a motorbike. John Maciver, son of Murdo from Breanais, must have learnt a lot from his father's biking days. His mechanical expertise must have extended beyond his motorbike because he went on to open an electrical shop in Steòrnabhagh in partnership with Fred Dart, a Londoner whom he met in the war.

From the summer of 1941 until November 1942 there was a considerable amount of activity on the Carnais to Mealastadh stretch of road. Gravel was quarried at Carnais for the buildings at the *Geodha Sgoilte*, Breanais and Mealastadh. All this heavy traffic on the roads, which after all were really made for a horse and cart, meant quite a lot of damage was caused. The men and boys who had found work on the buildings, continued in paid employment repairing the roads. The War Department provided the money and the men provided the muscle. It was all '1 RB' (pick and shovel) stuff, with much of the material for filling holes coming from the small quarry at the Mangurstadh shore road.

The money earned on this wartime work also opened up a whole new world to an almost 16-year-old Iain *Tobaidh* Macdonald. He was able for the very first time in 1941 to afford the bus fare to Steòrnabhagh. The furthest he had ever been was Bhaltos for his holidays, and occasional visits to his grandfather's in Geisiadar. It was mid-June when he set off on *Sgail's* bus for his trip into the Great Unknown. For two hours he was able to marvel at the new scenery and when eventually the bus arrived at the stands in Bayhead he just stood transfixed. Recalling the experience he said he was, "goggle-eyed at the people, the cars! Cor blimey, a country yokel found it hard to take in! Nowadays you go to Steòrnabhagh to be born. I waited nearly 16 years before tasting the delights of the big city! But after that I went as often as I could."

To Paradise and Back on *Sgail's* Bus

John *Sgail* Macaulay of No.8 Islibhig drove his Commer bus to Steòrnabhagh two or three days a week. He started the run in the early 1930s, taking over from Murdo Macaulay of No.5. Islibhig. He was a man with a quick wit and an amazing ability to forecast the weather accurately. Being a big man, he struck a splendid pose in his Harris tweed plus fours. In 1944 due to failing eyesight he sold the bus run to John Mitchell who was always quick to spot a niche in the market. When the Uig boys returned on Leave they invariably sent a telegram ahead of them to the police in the hope that an Uig bus would meet them from the boat. In wartime the timing of the boat was all over the place and all too often they would be stranded in Steòrnabhagh. To cater for this Mitchell's bus left Breanais at 1pm, arrived in Steòrnabhagh at 3pm and waited for the boat before returning to Breanais. This service continued until 1947 with the bus being driven, from 1945, by a very young Norman Macaulay.

Peter Macritchie of Eadar Dhà Fhadhail was renowned for his dry wit, amiable disposition, and incredible patience. He started his bus run in the 1920s and continued until 1950. He was a tailor by trade, hence his Gaelic name *an Taillear*. Some days there would be five buses on the Uig-Steòrnabhagh run but the population was high and the buses were only fourteen seaters. One of these bus operators was Iain *Sheogaidh* Maclean of An Aird and the others were Murdo Mackay of Bhaltos and Angus Mackay of Cairisiadar. Peter's bus, a Bedford, ran five days a week. Wednesdays were half-closing in Steòrnabhagh so he drove his grocery van around the district on that day. He often finished his round in the early hours of Thursday morning.

The bus would leave Breanais at 8.30am and along the route would be waiting either passengers or those wanting messages. Peter noted each person's order in a notebook and purchased the items during the day charging about a shilling extra for his time and no one begrudged him this. He also collected eggs from various people and delivered these to the Royal Hotel. He never passed a child on the road without giving them a free lift and a handful of sweeties. The first task of the day for most of the male passengers was a quick dram at The Lewis and Peter invariably paid for the round.

The bus would be at the stand on North Beach at 6pm but not all the passengers would be there on time. It was Peter's job, as he saw it, to take back all the passengers that he brought in so the stragglers had to be found. He never left anybody behind but many of them were loath to leave the bars of The Lewis and the old Crown Inn. They all knew what a patient man he was and they all took full advantage! He did the rounds, dragging many a well-oiled Uigeach reluctantly away from the warmth and conviviality.

Those who travelled into Steòrnabhagh at the rear of the bus had to find other places for the return journey because the back seats were usually removed to accommodate the sacks of oatmeal, flour and other bulky items. There were always discharged accumulators on the outward run and charged ones on the return.

The length of the trip back to Breanais depended on where the passengers stayed, what had to be unloaded along the route, how many stops there were for a "quick one" at someone's house, and, of course, there were a number of unofficial stops for those passengers with excess liquid on board! Sometimes it was 11pm or later before Peter managed to get everyone and everything delivered safely.

The journey to the Grioarstadh gate was fairly comfortable and quick due to the tarmac surface, although Peter was no 'speed merchant'. After that it was much slower on the narrow and winding gravel road and there were gates to open and close at each township. In the dry spells the progress of the bus could be traced from miles away by the clouds of dust surrounding it.

All good things must come to an end and so in 1948 Iain *Tobaidh* converted from his BSA bicycle and the bus to a 350 Panther motorbike which cost him £25. Fuel could be obtained from Miabhaig where Cyril Gooch had installed a hand operated pump in the 1930s. Then in 1949 Iain gave his Panther to his brother and set off to the mainland, worked for a short time on the dam at Mulardoch and eventually arrived in Leith, Edinburgh and signed on for eighteen months to work in the whaling industry, South Georgia. When he returned in 1951 the Uig road had been tarmac-ed all the way to the Breanais turning point. He drove his newly purchased Triumph 350 motorbike on the new road surface (*s'math sin*). For another five years he braved the elements in oilskins, gauntlets, and goggles (essential in summer) but inevitably went soft. In 1947 he bought himself a 1947 Morris Minor van for £90.

Since the 1950s the road has gradually improved. Long stretches from Gearraidh na h-aibhne have been rebuilt, some single track, some double and an expensive bridge now spans the river at Ceann Lochroag. In some places the old road lies deep beneath a considerable thickness of tarmac. Nowadays, there are many fewer heart-stopping blind summits and bends with their tell-tale black tyre stripes. It is now possible to drive from Breanais to the Co-op in less time than it takes to get through the tills there, on a Friday afternoon!

1934 Bedford 12 seater bus

1934 - Bus an Tailear in Ardroil

Photo Courtesy © Pat Macdonald

Falbh a' Chladach

The bays of *Tamana Siar, Mol Linnis, Mol Forsgeo, Breanais, Shiobachd, Islibhig* and *Mangurstadh* seem to attract more than their fair share of debris. Some of it comes from passing ships or fishing boats, some from distant and local coastal activities, and some from thousands of miles away. All the things that end up on the shore are the passive victims of the currents, winds, and tides.

In the early 1940s any number of planks came ashore and many of the *geodhs* were choked with them. These were quickly sorted through by the Upper-Enders and the good, clean, undamaged ones were pulled above high water mark, stacked and weighed down with a large stone or two. The tarry, broken and split ones, were very generously left for those in the Lower End of the parish. However, despite the rule about stuff above high-water mark being already claimed, there was many a 'clean' plank spirited away from the stacks by visitors in the night. Far fewer of these precious timbers came ashore in the rest of the parish.

The teenage Iain *Tobaidh* and his friends would regularly wander the strandline in the early 1940s, to replenish their supply of cigarettes. The metal cans of Players and Capstan were waterproof and each one held 50 smokes. Any amount of them could be gathered. Very highly prized by the boys were the American Care Ration packs. These contained tins of condensed milk, Horlicks tablets and chocolate biscuits, as well as cigarettes. There were also boxes of butter and fat and, if you scraped off the outside, the middle was perfectly good to eat. There were barrels of gear and lubricating oil which was good for the looms and other machinery.

UIG DURING THE WAR YEARS

The RAF Camps

The Second World War brought many changes to Uig and none more so than at the Upper End. After war was declared, young men and some women volunteered or were called up for active service and these people endured life-changing experiences. Some sacrificed their lives, and some were permanently disabled. Families were disrupted and crofts lost essential workers. Veterans of the First World War and anyone over sixteen joined the Local Defence Volunteers. They drilled and practised shooting their 303 rifles on the machair at Eadar Dhà Fhadhail, under the command of Capt. Duncan Maciver.

RAF Breanais and RAF Islibhig were part of the radar defence system installed around the coast of the British Isles. In the summer of 1941 this significant change to the townships of the Upper End of Uig began happening. Lorries appeared in Breanais and Mealastadh and a team of men began putting pegs in the ground. This alarmed some crofters because the pegs were in the middle of their potato patches but to the delight of all, jobs were offered to everyone. Boys under eighteen who, to this day, swear that they had to work harder than the men, got eleven pence ha'penny per hour and the men got 1/6. The contractors were Simpson Cooke of Nottingham.

There were concrete bases to lay, roads to build and Nissen huts to be erected. At Mealastadh there were to be nine Nissen huts, two gantries for the masts, an air-raid shelter and some wooden buildings. Nissen huts came as complete kits with sheets, windows, nuts and bolts etc. Gravel for the concrete was quarried by hand at Carnais close to the bridge (this was the start of gravel quarrying in

Carnais). To everyone's relief no work took place in the potato patches until after lifting time. Flight Sergeant Blundell ran an unofficial bar and you could get a "screw top" filled from the 35-gallon keg for a shilling.

The Breanais buildings took a little longer to complete and were the main barracks, with some of the huts interlinking to make a dining hall with a stage. Another group of huts were linked to make the NAAFI. These were sited around the area that is now used as the Breanais sheep fank. Across the road were the Officers' quarters. There were about thirty huts, three air raid shelters and a powerhouse with Crossley engines and a generator.

Further huts were constructed at the *Geodha Sgoilte* where there was also a radar scanner with the electronics hut protected by blast-proof walls. All these installations were manned by two hundred or more RAF personnel, mainly British, with a fair number of New Zealanders and Canadians. The guards were army personnel of the Cameron Highlanders and they lived at Mealastadh and at the *Geodha Sgoilte*. The RAF boys went up in vehicles to do their watches.

In November 1942 there was a memorable day. With their pockets full of hard-earned cash, the Home Guard members dressed in their uniforms and presented themselves at the newly opened NAAFI bar. Calum Buchanan No.11 Breanais declared the refreshment to be the best beer he had ever tasted. It was specially brewed strong ale and was sold for 10d (old pence) a pint. The bar was only open to servicemen and ex-servicemen, and women never attended. Shortly after this momentous event dances and film shows began. These happened every two weeks in the dining hall which soon got the nickname 'The Breanais Odeon'. A fifteen-year-old Neil Latimer, who had come from Glasgow, was the expert and he was able to fill in everyone on the latest news of the 'filums' and the actors and actresses. The film shows and dances were attended by anyone from their teens to thirty or more. A gramophone or local musicians provided the music.

The dances were especially attractive to the thirty or so young women of the district. Peggy Murray never felt lonely or isolated at the school at Mangurstadh road-end and Katie Anne Macritchie No.12 Eadar Dhà Fhadhail fondly remembers the arrival of the lorry that took them to the dances and returned them safely home afterwards. The NAAFI had its attractions for the young men, being staffed with girls from Nis, An Ruadh and Cradhlastadh. Incidentally, many of them subsequently married locally. The manageresses came from the mainland, but some were more local. Murdina Campbell was from Nis and she later married Malcolm Mackinnon No.18 Breanais.

There were also ENSA (Entertainments National Service Association) concert parties who stayed for two weeks and were then replaced by another group. There were usually three men and three women who sang, played instruments, and performed sketches.

News of the progress of the war was listened to on the wireless. These were wired up to accumulators which were charged at the camp. However, almost the only people who had wirelesses were those with a disability, such as blindness or partial deafness. There was one at the Browns house, No.7 Islibhig, and there was another at No.6 Breanais, the home of two bachelors, which served as the men's *taigh cèilidh*. Listeners were warned in advance of important speeches and announcements that would be broadcast at 9.30pm. A dozen or so would crowd round the set to hear Winston Churchill's latest stirring words. The radio station at Mangurstadh was a naval communications installation.

This opened in 1943 but there was no NAAFI or facilities for locals at that site until after the war.

The end of hostilities did not mean that the camps closed immediately but VE night did mean that all rules were relaxed. In the dance hall alcohol was consumed and women were served in the bar. Fortunately for Iain *Tobaidh*, he just happened to be On Leave and was able to take full advantage, recalling that, "the night was well worth remembering, I'll tell you", he recalled

There was a gradual demob of personnel until the camps at the far end of the parish closed in the summer of 1946 and the buildings were left empty. The Crossley engines at the Breanais powerhouse were transferred to Mangurstadh where they replaced the Caterpillar engines. According to Iain, there was also a certain amount of 'beachcombing on the QT'. The windows were no good because they had frosted glass but doors, partitions and floorboards were 'liberated'. In July 1947 there was an auction of the remains.

Mangurstadh was transferred from the Navy to the Ministry of Civil Aviation and a bar and cinema opened in 1946. Once again Iain *Tobaibh* and Peter Macleod at No.4 Mangurstadh were able to attend the opening. The Highlands and Islands Film Guild sent over films to be shown every two weeks. The showings alternated between Cradhlastadh School and Mangurstadh station.

Although life during the war years was severe for some, others found it more pleasant. Rationing of food hardly affected people in Uig. Their mail was all censored as the islands were Restricted Areas but for many there was more money than they had ever seen. They could buy 'exotic' foods at the NAAFI store and the 'entertainment' which had been, at most, three dances a year in Breanais School was almost unlimited.

Mealastadh where the remains of the RAF camps are still visible.

Geodha Sgoilte RAF camp – remains of the air raid shelter

A Lucky Strike in Breanais

On the afternoon of 7th May 1943, Iain *Tobaidh* was at Macritchie's shop in Eadar Dhà Fhadhail and it was sunny, not cold, but there were occasional hail squalls. Standing outside the shop, he and Calum Morrison of No.8 Mangurstadh watched a large aircraft circle Uig sands a couple of times and then set off in a southerly direction. They thought nothing more of it. Later Iain pedalled his bike back home only to find the enormous aircraft on the ground south of the croft.

His parents had been planting oats when the plane came very low over Islibhig. They thought it would land on their croft but to their relief it touched down just beyond the boundary and slid to a halt on Breanais ground. The propellers were bent and the belly-turret was torn off but otherwise there was very little damage. Minutes after it landed, some RAF personnel from the Breanais camp approached the stricken aircraft, only to see that the guns of the front turret were trained on them.

The B17 *Flying Fortress* was a USAAF YB-40, a new and special type of B17 designed to protect bomber squadrons when they raided over Germany. They were equipped with extra guns and radar jamming devices and were therefore top secret. The crew had left Goose Bay in Labrador and flown south of Greenland but had failed to pick up radio contact. Their instructions were to return to Goose Bay under such circumstances, but they decided that they had sufficient fuel to take them to Meeks Field in Iceland. At this time the Germans had set up radio transmitters in Norway, in order to give a false radio signal. This was to disrupt the navigation of these American aircraft as they were delivered on the *North Atlantic Ferry*. (Over 20,000 aircraft made the crossing during the war). The solid cloud cover meant that they could not see Iceland, but they circled for an hour without managing to establish a radio fix. Eventually they decided to make for Steòrnabhagh, wherever that was. With fuel supplies running low, they were well and truly lost.

When they finally emerged from the storm clouds, they sighted hills and large sea lochs, giving them the impression that they were over Norway. Reluctantly after twelve hours and fifty minutes in flight, and the fuel situation getting desperate, they circled a sandy bay before spotting a flat area of peatland to the south. They thundered in over a small village, noticed people working in the fields, skimmed over their heads and managed a perfect, wheels-up landing, with no injury to any person or to any of the many cows that were grazing on the moor. As far as they were concerned their war was almost over before it had begun. Norway was occupied by the enemy. As they came to a halt and recovered their senses, they saw several 'grey' uniformed personnel running towards them. Immediately they manned their half-inch machine guns and decided to make a fight of it. They would certainly take a few Germans with them before they were themselves killed or captured.

The RAF boys had recognised the aircraft as 'friendly' and were running to aid a crew who they thought might have been injured. Fortunately for them, before an itchy American finger squeezed the trigger, they realised that they were looking down the barrels of a machine gun. Shouted warnings and commands were recognised in the plane as being English voices. Was this an elaborate German trick? It took some time to convince the Yanks that everybody was on the same side.

Then there was an excited seventeen-year-old Iain on his bike as well as residents of Islibhig and Breanais arriving to greet the heroes from over the 'pond'. The pilot, First Lieutenant Paul Casey was, according to Iain, a "pint-sized fellow" and his brilliant flying skills had rescued the whole mission from disaster. It was he and his crew who introduced the local lads to the delight of smoking a Lucky Strike cigarette while sitting in the cockpit imagining themselves on a bombing raid over Germany. Later in the afternoon a USAAF jeep arrived from Steòrnabhagh with a "big shot" officer. The crew of the "Fort" were lined up for inspection and congratulations on a "damn good job".

Over the next few weeks, a track was constructed out to the aircraft that can still be seen today running west from the road, just north of the old school in Breanais. The four engines and the wings were removed using electric arc-welders, much to the amazement of the locals. The fuselage was the first piece to leave. It was on a trailer pulled by a four-wheel drive Studebaker with a jeep behind attached to the tail wheel by an iron bar. By this method they steered this cumbersome load along the rough and ready road to Steòrnabhagh. They left Breanais soon after midday and arrived in Steòrnabhagh sometime after nine the next morning, having had a severe problem at the narrow bridge at *Cist an Fhors'*. Note: this land journey took eight hours longer than the flight across the Atlantic!

D-Day and VJ Day

We owe a great debt of gratitude to quite so many *Uigeachs* who took part in the events of D-day all those years ago. There were seven *Uigeachs* directly involved. Iain Macdonald of Giosla, a piper in the Seaforth Highlanders, who was the youngest boy in the family, sadly lost his life near Caen. Calum Buchanan of Breanais was with the Gordon Highlanders while Iain Smith of Eadar Dhà Fhadhail and Kenny Macdonald of An Riof were in the Seaforths. All three were wounded in Northern France. Iain Murdo Macdonald of Bhaltos, was on HMRT Emphatic and Iain Macdonald of Islibhig, was on HMRT *Samsonia*. These two tugs were used to tow sections of Mulberry Harbours to the Normandy beaches. Calum Morrison of Mangurstadh was on ML10, a motor launch and was part of a decoy force sent to Dieppe and Calais. They were expected to be a sacrificial force but fortunately they suffered very few casualties. All these young men were heroes, even though they would always say that they were only doing their duty.

However, one of them was lucky not to be on a charge for a serious breach of security. It involved Calum *Nelson* Morrison, Iain *Tobaidh* and Iain's mother. Fortunately, the sharp-eyed censor made sure that no enemy agent lurking around Islibhig would get to know where Iain *Tobaidh* was.

It happened that while anchored off the Arromanches beaches Iain was amazed to see a rowing boat approaching his tug from a motor launch moored nearby. On board was *Nelson* paying him a social call. Later Iain wrote home, as he regularly did, but he was always careful not to mention where he was or what he was involved in because this was strictly against the rules. In his letter he happened to mention that he had seen *Nelson* recently. The censor assumed that the 'Nelson' referred was the battleship *HMS Nelson* that was stationed off the Normandy beaches at the time. That offending but innocent snippet of news had been completely blanked out when the letter eventually arrived in Islibhig.

On 15th August 1945 there were some very relieved young men from the Upper End. There had been great festivities in May to celebrate the end of hostilities in Europe but unfortunately that did not mark the end of the fighting or misery for everyone.

Iain *Tobaidh* was on board the rescue tug *Samsonia* in Falmouth harbour ready to sail for the Far East at any time. On 15th August the crew were given 48 hours leave followed by another 48 hours and then the dockworkers came on board and started to remove the guns and ammunition lockers. It was all over: they would not be sailing!

John Murdo and Angus Maclean, and Murdo Morrison of Breanais, and Donald Buchanan of Mangurstadh, were all serving on ships in the Pacific and braving suicide attacks from desperate Japanese pilots. Norman *Sudraidh* Macleod was deep in the jungles of Burma with the Chindits – part of the 'Forgotten Army'. He was called up in 1942 and was posted to Burma. His 'talents' were soon recognised by Orde Wingate. He was able to hide very effectively; probably a skill learnt in his youth. Many people in Uig will testify to his remarkable ability of disappearing before your very eyes, and that was not in the jungle, but on the moor. In certain circumstances this was a very useful skill indeed. In Burma he was sent ahead to 'scout' settlements and villages for the enemy before the main patrol advanced. The Chindits fought behind enemy line and were made up of Ghurkha, Burmese, and British personnel. Their job was to sabotage the enemy supply lines and cause maximum disruption to the Japanese forces. Some described the conditions as like being in absolute hell. There were Japanese troops everywhere. They were constantly wet from rain, from wading through swamps or permanently damp with sweat. Many suffered from recurrent bouts of typhus and malaria. Before the war ended *Sudraidh* had been promoted to Patrol Leader. Although they did not suffer the same horrors and privations as the POWs, the Chindits were certainly having a hard time of it and were very pleased when hostilities ended.

During that August, Kenny Maclean of No.1 Breanais was desperately clinging on to life. He was very weak from starvation and illness. He was convinced that he was destined for the hospital tent and knew there was only one way out of there: in a box. In 1942 he was a member of the crew of *HMS Stronghold* which was an 'S' class destroyer fitted out as a minesweeper. In the wake of the disastrous Battle of the Java Sea, the skipper and crew were attempting to escape to Australia 'to fight another day'. However, fuel was low and there was an argument between the skipper and chief engineer. Eventually they decided to proceed at half-speed rather than become stranded in mid-ocean. It turned out to be the wrong choice and soon the Japanese heavy cruiser *Maya*, and the destroyers *Arashi* and *Nowake* overtook them. On March 2nd 1942 the *Stronghold* was sunk and 50 men died. Most of the 40 survivors ended up on the Maya as prisoners. The Commander warned them that his respectful and kindly treatment of them as fellow sailors would not be acceptable to the army who would be in charge once they reached land. They were off-loaded in the Celebes. This was the start of three and a half years of starvation, torture and illness. The details of Kenny's ordeal will never be known because he was reluctant to tell – the memories must have been all too painful. Needless to say, the 15th August did not come a day too soon for him.

Meanwhile 2,500 miles away a neighbour of Kenny's, Malcolm Morrison No.16 Breanais was even more relieved when the Japanese surrendered. A couple of days earlier orders had been issued for his execution but the sentence had not yet been carried out. He had joined the Seaforth Highlanders on 12th April 1934 and served in Palestine, Egypt and Hong Kong before arriving in the British sector of the International Settlement in Shanghai. Here he had been persuaded to leave the army and joined the Shanghai Police Force. In September 1939 he asked to re-join the army but the authorities wanted him to stay in the police, to prevent the loss of Shanghai to the Japanese, who were occupying much of China at the time. Unfortunately, this arrangement became untenable in early 1942 when the Japanese declared war on the Allies. He immediately became a 'political' prisoner, which turned out to be a far worse status than being a POW. At first, he was held in Shanghai, but later he was moved to Nanking. He was regularly taken out for beatings and torture. On one occasion his ordeal lasted five days. He was returned to the compound in an unconscious state and later was unable to explain to the medical orderly how he had received his terrible injuries. His feet were so badly damaged that for the rest of his life he refused to remove his socks in public. In the second week of August 1945, he was taken away and did not return at all. Fortunately for him the surrender intervened and he was discovered shortly after 15th August in a tiny cell awaiting execution by firing squad. Although he suffered bouts of ill health for the rest of his life he joined the army again and served for some years in Libya, reaching the rank of Captain. Eventually he moved to Dundee and worked for the Health Board until retirement.

Iain *Tobaidh* discovered another ex-POW of the Japanese. Duncan *Post* Macritchie's father, *a Niseach,* was one of the unfortunate prisoners 'employed' on the notorious Burma railway. He survived the experience but in common with Kenny and Malcolm, the memory of the horrors he suffered and witnessed never left him.

1944 - Iain Tobaidh & Calum "Nelson" Morrison

1945-46 - Bermuda

February 1945 – New York City
souvenir photo at Riverside Bar & Grill, 812, 8th Avenue

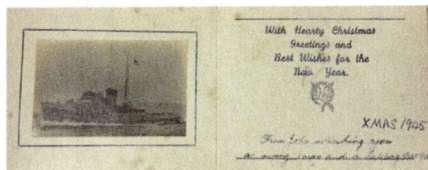

1945 - Christmas card home from
HMAS Samsonia

*1999 - Iain at Remembrance Service at
Uig War Memorial*

A WORKING LIFE

At the Whaling in South Georgia

After the War, with little in his pockets but a thirst for adventure, Iain *Tobaidh* Macdonald of Islibhig, recalled a job that he had carried out in September 1945, as a crew member of the tug HMRT *Samsonia*. A Norwegian whaling factory ship had been captured by the Germans in the South Atlantic. It was beached in the River Seine near Honfleur after having been attacked by RAF bombers. The job was to tow it to Rouen for repairs. Also on the crew of the *Samsonia* was a young Shetlander called Willie Hughson. He had excited young Iain with tales of his relatives spending a season or two in the Antarctic working at one of the whaling stations in South Georgia.

In August 1949, Iain gave his pride and joy, a 350 Panther motorbike, to his brother then packed a few essentials and set off for the Christian Salvesen's offices in Leith, Edinburgh to sign on for the whaling in South Georgia. Standing in the queue, he was amazed to hear from behind him a familiar voice say, "Iain Macdonald I presume." It was Willie Hughson who was, by then, an old hand at whaling, having done a couple of seasons already. They sailed down together on a transport ship from Greenock, and with a three day stop in Tenerife, they arrived a month later at Leith Harbour, South Georgia, where Iain was to spend the next eighteen months. Most of the men at the whaling station were Norwegians but there were also many Shetlanders and Geordies, as well as about eighteen Lewismen. Cabin 26 was Gaelic speaking, slept six in three bunks, but only one of them was an *Uigeach*.

They worked twelve-hour shifts seven days a week, and were paid £24 a month. Iain spent most of his time in the meat factory, 6am to 6pm, where the whale meat was boiled to extract the oil, cooked, and ground up, before being dried and bagged. Bones were also boiled and reduced to meal.

In the winter about thirty percent of the personnel were retained and the work was lighter, working from nine to five. The jobs were mainly maintenance work and painting. The winter, which was in our summer, was very cold and dark. Everything froze up and instead of the trolleys running on narrow gauge rails, sledges had to be used to move things about. In the season, whale meat was served on Saturdays, cooked with onions and "tasted just like steak."

Another of the delicacies on the menu was penguin eggs. They were twice the size of a hen's egg and served up once a week in the canteen. The 'white' of their eggs was a pale blue colour. Salted and corned beef from Argentina and reindeer meat from the herd kept on the island were also served regularly. Pigs were also kept for their meat. There was fresh bread baked every day and fish caught locally. Every three weeks there was a bottle of rum for a cabin of six which, as you can imagine, did not last very long. At Christmas and New Year there were also bottles of beer.

Every week Iain sent two pounds ten shillings back home to his parents but the rest was saved - although there were the delights of the "slop chest" to spend money on. It was an Aladdin's Cave of oilskins, long johns, tobacco, sweets, toothpaste etc. The only other expense was the cinema where two or three films were shown each week.

The "big shots" around the place were the gunners. They were all Norwegians and were also captains of their catcher ships. They were paid big bonuses for the number of whales caught and most of them liked their drink. Iain commented, "A Norwegian can drink a Lewisman under the table anytime." One of the top gunners for Christian Salvesen, who incidentally was teetotal himself, was Juel Engebretsen, who lived at Macaulay Farm near Steòrnabhagh. A captain of one of Salvesen's tankers was Captain Swanson, who tragically died of a perforated ulcer and is buried in Leith Harbour, South Georgia. His daughter, Kay Gillies lived in Breanais at one time.

One of the winter jobs that Iain was required to do was to visit another whaling station, at Prins Olaf Harbour. This had been the Lever Brothers Antarctic base but in 1931, during the Depression, they pulled out of whaling altogether. Christian Salvesen immediately bought the station to prevent anyone else setting up in competition. At Prins Olaf were some dry-docks and the derelict buildings on land. The job was to demolish some of the buildings and bring salvageable parts back for re-use at Leith Harbour. In the powerhouse, written on one of the steel beams Iain was amazed to see a reminder of home. Painted in large letters was: 'Harris whaling station West Loch Tarbert 1920.'

May 1951 marked the end of the season and Iain returned home with £1100 in his pocket. Work was to be done back in Islibhig, building a new house at No 1 but he fully intended to return to South Georgia as soon as he could. The first thing he did when he got back was to spend £62 on a Triumph 350 motorbike. After all a young man needed transport!

Of his time in South Georgia Iain commented: "All in all, life was good and once a whaler always a whaler. The comradeship was good, and you spoke your own language." Between 1952 and 1957 the new No.1 house was built and Iain's plans were to sign on for another Antarctic stint but tragedy struck in December 1956. Iain's brother Murdanie was killed in Mangurstadh, and South Georgia became just a fond memory.

1949 – Leith Harbour, South Georgia

1949 – Murdanie Macdonald,
Iain's younger brother

1950 – Iain at home
from South Georgia

Penguins

One summer, there was the news of a king penguin at Edinburgh Zoo being awarded a knighthood by King Harald of Norway. The house at No.1 was turned upside down in search of a photograph taken nearly 59 years ago at Leith Harbour, South Georgia.

On the right is a very youthful Iain Macdonald and on the left his friend, Donald Murray of Siabost. In the middle is a very friendly king penguin. The photograph was taken close to the whaling station. The penguins were very tame and wandered freely round the town.

It was easy to approach the penguins but if you picked one up you had to watch it! Their wings could hurt and you had to keep your face away from their beaks. They were a dead weight, and you couldn't hold them for long. They were interesting characters. When they came out of the sea, about twenty or more would gather in a circle. One was often in the middle – just like a village meeting. Then that one would move out of the circle and another one would take its place. They were comical birds, quite slow on land but in the water they were too fast for the leopard seals.

On the way home after his eighteen months in the Antarctic, Iain often went to look at the penguins on the deck. Christian Salvesen usually took some penguins back for European zoos. They were kept in pens, and had a bad time when the ships neared the Tropics. Inevitably, some died but most of them survived. It is quite likely that the ancestor of the penguin that was recently knighted was originally from South Georgia.

Weaving the Tweed

One late summer the weather was beautiful and I decided to paint the outside of the house. Balancing precariously on the fully extended ladder, I was struggling to get the paint into all the nooks and crannies of the roughcast. Drifting to my ears from time to time was not just the sound of flies buzzing, lapwings calling or the occasional bleat of a sheep, but another, mechanical and rhythmic sound. At first, I wasn't sure what I was hearing. It was a sound that my brain told me was familiar but which I hadn't heard for some time: a sound that pervaded every village at one time but which nowadays it is rarer than the call of the corncrake in summer. In recent times there were only a few places in Uig where the sound could still be heard: in Islibhig, Miabhaig, Cradhlastadh and Bhaltos. This particular day I knew the sound was from the south, because the breeze told me so. This breeze is the same one that in June, after the fisherman's visit, used to bring, to Islibhig, the smell of fresh herring being fried in Breanais. Anyway, it eventually dawned on me that the clackety-clack of the loom at No.1 Islibhig was the sound I was hearing. There was a time when almost every croft had a loom shed from which emanated this busy sound. Inside each shed there was a Hattersley Domestic Semi-Automatic Treadle Loom, and the money earned from the tweeds it produced once paid most of the household bills. Some homes had as many as three looms; the crofter, his wife and at least one of their offspring would all weave, and when there were tweeds, the money would come "peddling-in"!

The first treadle powered loom did not appear in the Upper End of Uig until 1936 or so. Murdo Maclean, No.1 was the first person in Breanais to buy a Hattersley loom. In Islibhig the first of these revolutionary machines appeared at No.1 in 1946 and Iain *Tobaidh* Macdonald had to pay the princely sum of £65 for it. His gratuity, and some money his father had earned working at Steòrnabhagh aerodrome, paid for it. Others bought their looms from Peter Macritchie, Eadar Dhà Fhadhail. Before the war you could buy a loom from him for £40, and when you were earning some money from the tweeds you could pay him back in instalments. (In 1980 a new Hattersley loom cost £6000). It didn't take Iain *Tobaidh* long to pick up the skills needed to keep the loom running smoothly. His father filled the bobbins for the shuttles using a converted spinning wheel but he had quite a job keeping up with the loom. Eventually in 1948 they bought a treadle powered bobbin winder for £14 and this could fill three bobbins at a time. A second-hand Japanese one-horsepower engine and an extra spindle were soon added (in 1954 the engine became redundant when the electric arrived).   The first tweed woven on the miraculous machine measured about 40 weaver's yards (a weaver's yard is 8 feet). This meant that the piece of cloth was well over 100 yards long (but only 29 inches wide when shrunk). For this Iain was paid £2-18-0, which was better than the 1/- a weaver's yard, paid in 1939. He could usually manage two or two and a half tweeds a week, depending on the croft work.

To house the new loom a shed had already been built. The walls were only one concrete block thick and there was no form of heating but as Iain explained: "Even in the coldest weather you didn't need it – the loom was the best heater of the lot." He spoke in a philosophical way about the pleasures of the loom and its significance as a source of income: "While you were weaving you never needed any entertainment, like they do nowadays. Once the loom was going you could disappear into your imagination. In your mind you could build castles in the air one day and knock them down the next. You were never short of company when you had your thoughts. If you did get a visitor, it was impossible to continue working because of the noise, but every minute you sat chatting, was your own money being wasted. Compare that to working on the roads, when time off for a chat was paid for by somebody else!"

Mid-1990s - Iain in his signature blue dungarees busy with a tweed

2004 – Iain filling the bobbins

2004 – Iain on his Hattersley Loom

The Weaver's Job

Each week two sacks would arrive from the mill in Steòrnobhagh on the local bus. The warp would be in one sack and the yarn for the weft was on large bobbins in the other. The warp had to be unplaited and passed over beams in the roof of the shed. The threads were separated into small bundles on a spiked gadget on the top of the loom, called the raddle and were then tied onto the beam. Slowly the beam was turned with a handle and the warp wound onto it. In the 1950s the occasional warp arrived ready wound onto a beam, which was very convenient. Eventually it was the norm for warps to arrive ready-beamed. A ticket sent with the yarn showed what pattern was to be woven. Sometimes this required the weaver to re-thread the warps through one heddle eye or another for example herringbone twill, plain weave and the like. Once this was done, the new warp threads were tied to the old warp threads which had been left in the loom from the last tweed. There was a maximum of 698 threads to tie in. Then the old warps were pulled through the heddles so that the new warp threads eventually came through the reed. A few 'peddles' helped to tension the warp threads. Pulling them, and hooking them onto the spiked take-up roller, tightened any slack threads. It was sometimes necessary to set a different order for the shuttles according to the wefting plan on the ticket. This was done by fitting the appropriate steel cards in the box chain.

The other sack was taken over to the bobbin winder. The machine was turned by a foot-treadle like a spinning wheel. It transferred the yarn from the large bobbins, supplied by the mill, to the small bobbins called pirns that fit into the shuttles. When everything was ready the shuttles were loaded with full pirns and put into the shuttle box. Sitting on a small stool behind the loom the weaver peddled away to get the tweed started. Immediately the weaving shed would be full of noise. The pick-sticks swung back and forth pulling leather straps that curled and slapped the picks which, in turn, flung the shuttle from side to side. The shuttles hurtled across the loom at 25mph, which is why there is such a loud 'clack' every time it was struck or when it entered the box. With each pass of the shuttle, the going part swung forward and the reed beat in the weft thread before the shed was reversed to trap it in the weave. Soon a few inches of tweed were woven at a rate of 80 to 140 picks a minute. Then everything was stopped to determine whether all the warps were in place and the pattern appeared regular and correct. It was essential that any problems were rectified at this stage; otherwise the tweed could have a fault running right the way through it. You were allowed so many faults but over a limit you were charged for repair time and this was deducted from your pay. In the early days there was a delay of up to ten days before you were paid. However, the Union negotiated a better system whereby you were paid within two days and any deductions were docked from your next pay. When everything looked OK the peddling recommenced and soon the loom settled into an easy rhythm, and those 'castles in the sky' could begin to appear. At the end of each day's weaving the shuttles were taken into the house and stored near the range. Left outside in the damp weaving shed they would swell, and then 'stick' when weaving started the next morning.

In 1963 Iain *Tobaidh* took on an 'unpaid but experienced' assistant in the loom shed. Having moved from Aird Bheag in 1953 and settled in Carnais in 1954, Ina Macdonald and her sister Peigi took up the noble art of weaving. They shared a loom which they got from Harris. Their neighbour Norman Morrison taught them the rudiments of the job. After her marriage, Ina became 'a legally bound assistant weaver' (otherwise known as a wife) at No.1 Islibhig, and she was able to take part in a famous record-breaking event.

This happened in 1964 - before there were distractions such as children. There was already a partly completed tweed on the loom when the young couple received another beam from Smiths Mill, marked VERY URGENT. Iain peddled furiously until the old tweed was completed. By about 6pm they had the new one tied in. Taking it in turns to fill bobbins and peddle the loom, the two of them toiled through the night. The loom hardly stopped for the thirteen hours it took to complete the tweed. It was then thrown into the Austin A30 and had to be driven down to John Matheson's bus at Miabhaig before he set off for Steòrnabhagh. Ina was in the passenger seat ready to prod her man in case he fell asleep at the wheel!

By 2004 when, up a ladder, I heard the sound of the loom working, Iain *Tobaidh* was the last remaining Harris Tweed weaver in Uig. He told me that he found it hard to get going on the first tweed of a batch. There were often many months between each delivery and new orders came without warning. Reluctantly all those threads must be tied in - although there was extra money for that task. The first half tweed would be done against his will because he would find himself remembering other important tasks that needed attending to. Eventually there would be an urgent call from the mill: "We need the tweeds before the end of next week!" This would certainly speed things up! The money was a welcome supplement to the pension, and the weaving work was a link to the past.

After 57 years of weaving, the tweeds Iain tied into his loom had to be collected from the mill in Steòrnabhagh and then delivered back when each was finished: at the time the mill no longer considered it profitable to deliver the beam and yarn to his home at No. 1 Islibhig.

The Outboard Motor

The weaving shed at No.1 Islibhig was always in the wrong place – anyone visiting could only be seen when his or her head appeared round the door. It would have been far too risky to fit an 'outboard' motor, the 'weaver's home help', even though it would have made life so much easier. (Of course, no one could add an electric motor until after 1952-54 because there was no electricity).

So using the covert 'outboard' was a strictly illegal operation - against all the Orb Mark regulations. When the Inspector arrived in the Lower End of the Parish he was soon spotted and the bush telegraph system got going. He would often park his car a short distance from a suspect loom-shed. The engine was turned off and the window wound down. It was said that he could tell from the rhythm of the nearby loom whether there were two human legs powering it or whether the Hydro Board was helping out. However, in Uig his skills were severely tested; either the advanced warning worked or no one in Uig was guilty! The Harris Tweed Association suspected that there were 'outboards' in Uig but no one was ever caught. In the early days the punishment was suspension from tweed weaving for a certain length of time. Later however, this penalty was tightened up, and suspension became a lifetime ban! The Association let it be known that there was always somebody being caught somewhere on the island. Those that did use them say that once the outboard was fitted it was very difficult to go back to peddling for a living.

When a tweed was completed it would be returned to the Steòrnabhagh mill on the bus. When the mill lorries started collecting the tweeds in 1948, the country bus owners lost a lot of business. They were getting 5/- a tweed. The weavers had to go to the bank in Steòrnabhagh with their chits to get paid but when the mobile bank started up that year, you got your money at the house. A weaver would sign up with one or two of the four mills in Steòrnabhagh, either Mackenzie's, Macdonald's, Smith's or Newall's.

You could also send your fleeces to the mill and get back the equivalent in spun yarn. This would be woven, and the tweed sold to a Small Producer who then sold it on to buyers on the mainland.

In 1953 an apprehensive Iain *Tobaidh* received a visit from the Carloway policeman. He had brought an order to attend court in Glasgow, with a travel warrant attached. Iain had sold one of the tweeds he had woven to an agent, Mr. Patrick Macfarlane of Steòrnabhagh. Along with two other tweeds, they had 'gone astray' at Maryhill Station on their way to a factory in South Shields, near Sunderland. Mr. Macfarlane, the Clerk from the Macbrayne's office in Steòrnabhagh, Iain *Tobaidh* and two other weavers caught the ferry to Kyle, and from there travelled down to Glasgow on the train. Their wait outside the Courtroom was with some of the most unsavoury characters in Glasgow, many of them sporting stitched-up razor slashes across their faces. In court each of the weavers in turn had to identify their own tweeds. The famous advocate Lawrence Dowdalls was defending the two men who were accused of the theft. During the lunch recess one of them nipped out to the Registry office to get married. During the afternoon Court proceedings, Mr. Dowdalls asked for leniency for a man who was newly married - only half an hour ago! The judge however had little sympathy. He pronounced that due to the defendant's appalling criminal record, he would be delaying his honeymoon for a period of two year, the maximum term the court could award! Incidentally, Mr. Macfarlane managed to clinch a deal, actually in the Courtroom, that day. The Harris Tweed jacket he was wearing had caught the eye of several court officials and when approached he agreed to obtain them some lengths of the particular tweed when he got back home. A few months later Iain *Tobaidh* was to see Lawrence Dowdalls again. This time it was in the Clachan Bar, Steòrnabhagh, where the barrister was having a quick dram, before going on to defend a couple of notorious North Lochs poachers.

OTHER ISLIBHIG CHARACTERS

Nurse Chrissie

Iain *Tobaidh* Macdonald was an expert on the weather. He based his understanding of Islibhig meteorology on the sayings of his father and the other Islibhig and Breanais *bodach*s of the day. Iain observed cloud patterns, wind direction, the shape and position of the crescent moon, and animal activity to help in predicting the weather. He had an amazing ability to recall the weather on specific days in the past. He also admitted to me that he would watch *Countryfile* on Sundays, for the long-range forecast. He was particularly interested in weather extremes, and vividly recalled the early months of 1947 and the way in which it affected lives in Uig.

I spent some time trawling through the Gazettes of 1947, becoming immersed in the events of that year, and how the weather affected various parts of Lewis. Fortunately, because of post war austerity, and the rationing of paper, the *Stornoway Gazette* at that time consisted of far fewer pages than it does today!

In one of the April papers, I came across a sad but nevertheless interesting record of a person who died in Islibhig. In the notice of her death, it was suggested that she was well-respected and a great loss to the people of the Upper End. Her name was Chrissie Macaulay, more generally known as Nurse Macaulay or Nurse Chrissie. She was the wife of Murdo *Doddle* Macaulay of No 5 Islibhig, and despite being a trained and very experienced nurse, she was not in fact employed as such in Lewis.

She was born Christina Morrison on 12th January 1889. Her father was Donald, a fisherman crofter of No.21

Breanais. He was a very active man with a quick wit, well known for his vigour and intellect. Her mother was Marion Buchanan. They were married on 1st February 1881, and had five children – Donald, Calum, John, Christina and Angus.

She started her education at Islibhig school which of course, was actually in Breanais. Her best friend at the school was Katie Ann Macleod who was later to become the wife of Angus Macdonald from Geishiadar and mother of Iain *Tobaidh* and his three siblings of No. 1 Islibhig.

As a teenager, Chrissie was courted by a boy called Murdo Macauley who was her contemporary at school. Chrissie was a bright, go-ahead girl who took after her father, and when old enough decided to enter the nursing profession, a vocation that eventually took her to London. Apart from occasional visits home, she spent over thirty years away from Uig, before returning for good at the age of 51. It could have been the bombing of London that prompted her to return home to Uig.

Murdo *Doddle* Macaulay who, as a young man had hoped to wed his sweetheart Chrissie, must have been very disappointed when she left Breanais to train as a nurse. Distance and time meant that nothing came of his desire. He himself spent many years in England doing whatever job came his way. Whether he went south to follow Chrissie, or even whether they met in England, I did not discover. However, in 1914 he was called up and he joined the Royal Engineers. After the war, when he was demobbed, Murdo decided to return to Islibhig to join his mother, his sister Ann and uncle Kenneth, at No.5 and 6. In the late 1930s his mother died. On the crofts there were the usual sheep and black cattle and they grew oats and potatoes on what are probably the best crofts in the township.

In 1940, Murdo was astonished to discover that Chrissie had come back home for good and very pleased to hear that she was still single! He started to court her all over again but this time with more success. Some say that it was Murdo's beautiful Aberdeen Angus cattle that won her round this time. The pair were married later in the year, and Chrissie quickly converted to the role of crofter's wife. However, despite her tweed skirts and aprons, there was still a lot of the sophisticated 'city girl' in her. For instance, every Sunday she turned out for church in the clothes that were fashionable in 1940s London. One Islibhig resident at the time recalled her looking like a little doll, with fine clothes and beautiful snakeskin shoes. There were quite a few girls in the village, and further afield, who admired and envied her stylish attire.

Nurse Chrissie was a very convenient and willing source of medical advice in the two villages. She was immediately accessible to Islibhig residents and not far away from the people of Breanais. The nearest official nurse was Nurse Macqueen at Mangurstadh road-end. Despite not being employed as a nurse, Chrissie never accepted payment or reward for her local services.

She did not confine her advice to medical matters alone for she took a great interest in the young people, especially the teenage girls, who found her wise words invaluable. Chrissie had such a wide experience of things, not just of the world beyond the townships of the Upper End, but from far away and from a big city. She also knew a lot about fashion and clothes.

Chrissie was a kind person who lavished care upon her husband, the cattle and anybody who came to the door. She was no shrinking violet either. In conversation she was always ready to offer an opinion, she had no fear in voicing it. If she disagreed with something on principle she was quick to say so and gave it extra emphasis by delivering it, not in her native Gaelic, but very forcefully in English. This was even more striking because instead of sounding like a local, she had a pronounced English accent. Her Gaelic, of course, had not been affected by her thirty years away from home.

She was her own person but she entered life on the croft and the community with energy, efficiency and ability. Every morning, without fail she would take a bowl of porridge next door to *Doddles's* aunt Flora. Flora lived at No 6. Incidentally Flora was the last Islibhig resident to go to the sheilings, and the ruins of her bothy can still be found at the foot of *Mealaisbhal*.

The year 1947 started badly with exceptionally low temperatures – then the deep snow arrived causing serious disruption to life in Uig. It was nearly three months before the thaw set in and life could return to normal. However, it was not long before Islibhig was plunged into deeper gloom. In mid-April Chrissie took a stroke with what the paper described as 'startling suddenness' and in the early hours of 17th she died. She was only 59 years old. It was a great shock and loss to Murdo and to the people of the Upper End. As the correspondent for the *Stornoway Gazette* put it:

> *Nurse Chrissie never refused a call for help. The people of the district owe her a great debt for all her kindness during the seven years since she came back to the district. She will be greatly missed by all.*

She was the perfect example of the sort of neighbourliness that kept the community going before there were support services for the remoter areas. Not long after Chrissie's death things began to change. First there was the arrival of the Welfare State with free medicine and unemployment payments, and later council-funded social and emergency services. These obviously make life much easier, but the need for neighbourliness and mutual support will always be important in such isolated places as Uig.

A New Kitchen for No.5

Iain *Tobaidh* had a prestigious memory and most of the time he was infallible. However, there was one story he told me, many years ago, about a dramatic incident that took place in Islibhig where he was unsure of the year it had happened. He and others who were involved thought it may have been sometime in the 1970s. It was such a significant event that I resorted to the library copies of the *Stornoway Gazette*, where I was sure it would have been reported. All I had to do was browse through the copies of the paper starting in 1970. I may have mentioned before what a monumental job it is to look through a decade of flimsy and torn copies of the *Gazette*. You do come across a lot of interesting stories, but that is not the point of the exercise. Anyway, it took my wife and me many hours to wade our way through well over 500 newspapers to no avail. There was absolutely no mention of any significant incident occurring in Islibhig during the period in question. As the event involved the fire brigade and the police I wondered if they would be able to help with a date but my enquiries yielded nothing. I know it happened, because everybody I spoke to told me what a dramatic event it was, but surprisingly no one at the time had deemed it worth recording.

You will recall that in 1947 Murdo *Doddle* Macaulay became a widower when his beloved Chrissie died unexpectedly. He struggled on but having become used to married life found himself lonely. In 1949 Annie Macdonald from Chirceboist in Beàrnaraigh arrived in Breanais as a home help. *Doddle* took a liking to Annie and within three months of her arriving they were married.

Their house was single storey and thatched and at the south end there was a lean-to kitchen. In 1954, grants were made available to crofters for house improvements and

Murdo and Annie decided to apply. Murdo knew immediately the person he wanted to do the renovation work: during the war, a builder from Sgalpaigh, Angus Macleod, was one of the men employed on the construction of the RAF camp in Breanais and Mealastadh. He had lodged with Murdo and Chrissie during the time he was working on the camp and they had become good friends. Angus agreed to do the work and started in late 1954. He built up the south end and made a gable and he moved the kitchen to the back of the house where he constructed a poured concrete extension with a corrugated asbestos roof and plasterboard lining inside. Access to the kitchen was through the back door of the original house where the walls were three feet thick. The new back door out of the kitchen faced north.

Murdo and Annie were very pleased with their new kitchen and fitted a peat-burning stove for cooking and hot water and a sink under the west-facing window. There was a south-facing window through which they could keep an eye on the rest of the village. They had a table and chairs and Murdo installed a comfortable armchair close to the stove where he could toast his toes and smoke his pipe. They also had a shelf on which stood a primus stove. This was the appliance most people used to heat water quickly especially in the morning. Although you needed methylated spirit to start it and paraffin as a fuel, the primus was more convenient than the peat stove, which was good for cooking on but in the morning took forever to boil water for a cup of tea. However, in 1952 many people had started using a new method of heating a kettle of water. Butane gas in metal cylinders was introduced to the district. The blue 15kg Calor gas cylinder had a valve screwed on the top and a rubber pipe leading the gas to a ring burner on a shelf above. At some stage Murdo and Annie had obtained a Calor gas ring and installed it in their kitchen. Some twenty years later it was this appliance that so nearly cost them their lives.

The fateful morning in question was definitely a Saturday and all my informants have now agreed it must have been in the autumn of 1975. Murdo and Annie were busy with their morning activities. Annie was doing something in the main house and *Doddle* was in the kitchen. Early morning tea had been late again that morning because the Calor gas had run out a few days before. They had managed to get a new cylinder delivered but unable to have it installed.

Murdo was impatient and decided to carry out the installation himself. In those days Calor gas bottles had a regulator with a left-hand thread and it seems that Murdo was unaware of this. Using the appropriate spanner he turned the nut in a clockwise direction until he considered that it must be tight enough. Unfortunately, a left-hand thread tightens in an anti-clockwise direction so when Murdo finished the job gas leaked from the loose regulator. Butane is heavier than air so it gravitated to floor level and began to spread out.

The smell should have alerted him, but Murdo was unaware of it as he sat back in his comfy chair and prepared to light his pipe. Fly their dog was sleeping by the warm stove. As the gas covered the floor area he must have breathed it in. Butane gas causes euphoria and drowsiness before asphyxiation so the dog was probably having a beautiful dream immediately before the gas layer reached the firebox of the stove. With a loud 'woomph' the whole kitchen was engulfed in flame. *Doddle* was singed all over and he completely lost his eyebrows but fortunately his clothing did not catch fire. He staggered to the back door and stumbled outside. The breeze blowing that morning was strong enough to fan the flames that soon caught the curtains at one of the windows and then spread to the furniture.

It was a regular thing for the Buchanans at No.3 to note when the curtains in the kitchen of No.5 were drawn. This informed them that the elderly couple next door were up and about. That morning though they saw flames instead of curtains. Then there was an ear-splitting explosion.

At No.1 Iain *Tobaidh* and his eldest son Donald were at the side of their house. When they glanced down the village they saw smoke at the back of No.5. To their astonishment the corrugated asbestos roof of the lean-to erupted into the air and an object flew out. It described a beautiful arc in the sky and landed 150 yards down the croft. Only then did they hear the explosion. It turned out that the heat of the fire had caused the gas cylinder to explode, ripping a gash in its side and launching it through the ceiling. It was lucky that *Doddle* got out when he did because the blast from the exploding cylinder would undoubtedly have killed him.

Young Donald was immediately sent to *Breanais* to raise the alarm. He set off on his trusty bike and pedalled furiously down the road to the Latimers at No. 28. At both No.1 and No.3 Islibhig, the reaction was to grab a pail or two and hurry down the road to No.5. Annie was standing rather pathetically at the south end of the house. She had been in the living room when the door blew in and smoke and flames followed. She quickly left the building by the front door, unsure about the whereabouts of *Doddle*. The open front door fed the kitchen fire with more oxygen. She saw, to her great relief, her husband standing staring, shocked and dazed at the inferno that was his kitchen.

Annie joined him but she was horrified. In the kitchen was her carefully hidden stash of money, hoarded over the weeks and months. Her bank was not in Steòrnabhagh; instead it was in the large cube-shaped biscuit tin in which she stored the oatmeal. Deep in the meal was a wad of notes, tightly secured with a rubber band. She couldn't leave it to be consumed by the fire so she decided to plunge into the flames to rescue her makeshift safe. Fortunately, she was firmly restrained by her neighbours who tried to persuade her that it was only money and not worth losing your life for. She was inconsolable but as she watched the flames and smoke billowing out of her back door she gradually became reconciled to the fact that her nest-egg was gone.

Though neither Murdo nor Annie were in any danger, the neighbours decided it was their duty, if they could, to save the house from total destruction, even if in the process, they could be injured or killed themselves. Someone had dialled 999 but everyone knew that by the time the Steòrnabhagh fire engine arrived, No.5 would be a burnt-out shell.

By now, there were enough men from the two Upper End villages to form a bucket chain from the burn, conveniently situated only 30 yards away. The night before there had been an early autumn frost but luckily it was not hard enough to slow the flow of water and soon, by the bucketful, water was being thrown through the kitchen doorway onto the flames. It was fortunate that the kitchen back door was positioned close to the doorway into the main house, because by throwing water into the kitchen, they were also preventing the fire moving through into the living room. Incidentally, when the house was undergoing extensive renovation in 1996, you could see both charred rafters and sarking, showing just how close the house had come to being completely gutted. It was the sheer determination of the neighbours that saved the day. Within an hour the fire was out, and only the interior of the kitchen had been destroyed. When the town firemen arrived there was nothing for them to do, other than inform the brave fire-fighters of the Upper End that they could have been electrocuted. Apparently throwing water from a metal bucket onto the fuse box by the back door could have been fatal! It also transpired that some of them could have been peppered by lead shot, because in a fire scorched cabinet just inside the living room, was a box of shotgun cartridges. Sadly, when they sifted through the charred debris on the kitchen floor, they found the remains of Fly the dog.

Annie was pleased that the fire was out but what of her money? In due course the blackened and buckled meal tin was retrieved from the ashes, and presented to her. Inside the tin the meal had formed a charcoal crust but deep down it was still raw, and nestling in its fireproof coating was the roll of notes, not even warm. Annie was overjoyed. A quick phone call to Murdo's nephews, the Maciver brothers, meant that by the evening there was electricity and an intact house, albeit without the kitchen.

There were heroics that day but no medals, not even a mention in the *Stornoway Gazette*. There were three important outcomes from this incident in Islibhig. Firstly, all those who heard about the fire, moved their gas cylinders outside. Secondly, it is probable that the event led to the decision to base a fire unit in Uig in 1976 and long may it survive. Thirdly, and most critically, Annie was forced to find a new hiding place for her savings.

No.5 Islibhig

No.5 Islibhig with the kitchen at back of house

Photos Courtesy of Google Maps and George Macdonald

Dr Beveridge, Nurse Macqueen and Aird Bheag

Every summer the 'road watchers' are thrown into confusion as the season gets under way and there are a whole new crop of vehicles passing that cannot be identified. Some of these summer visitors are discovering the place for the first time while others were born here and are visiting friends and relations. There are yet others who are returning to a location that they know well, and have such great affection for, that many years later they feel the urge to return. In June one year, an elderly holidaymaker was reacquainting herself with some of her old haunts. In particular she wanted to visit a place she remembered well from an incident that happened there 54 years before.

In August 1952, she had been the doctor deputising for Dr. Matheson. The nurse had received an urgent call from John Macdonald of Aird Bheag. He had walked to Ceann Loch Rèasort from his home, as he did three times a week to collect and deliver the mails. He sent word via Malcolm Macaskill the Morsgail postie that medical assistance was needed at Aird Bheag. His wife Jessie was ill and was too poorly to travel overland, or even by boat. Nurse Macqueen, who was responsible for the Upper End of Uig, received the message and called on Dr. Beveridge, the young doctor who was on duty at the time. It was evening by the time the doctor picked up the nurse at Mangurstadh road end and they drove on to *Mol Linnis* hoping that there would be a boat waiting for them at the landing point. Dr. Beveridge was looking forward to the nocturnal adventure whereas the nurse was definitely not!

The boat was ready for them with a crew of the best boatmen in Breanais. They were Calum Iain *Bachan* Macaulay, Neil Angus Morrison, Kenny *Phoint* Maclean and Calum

Lornie Buchanan. It was a fine night, there was very little swell running, and there was enough light to see the shore. It was always safer at night to keep close to the shore to navigate and keep an eye out for the rocks. However, the disadvantage was the backwash which could make for an uncomfortable ride. This didn't trouble the crew, nor was it a problem to the young doctor, but poor Nurse Macqueen was soon turning very green, as the boat pitched and rolled. To make matters worse, as they approached the landing at Aird Bheag, the nurse stood up in the boat, too eager to get to dry land. She ended up lying in the bilges with her legs in the air! Even on 'terra firma' things didn't improve and the poor nurse was too ill to partake in the feast that had been prepared after the consultation. She was also, no doubt, anxious about the return boat journey. Ina and her sister Peigi were both at home at the time and Ina remembers the occasion very clearly. Sadly, the prognosis for Jessie Macdonald, Ina's mother, was not good and later she had to be taken to the hospital in Steòrnabhagh.

By a stroke of luck, Ina got word of the said Dr. Beveridge's return visit (with her husband and a cousin) to *Mol Linnis*, the landing place, 54 summers on.

Iain *Tobaidh* and Ina were able to meet them and chat over the 1952 emergency visit to Aird Bheag, when Ina was still a teenager.

This was not the only time that Nurse Macqueen was forced to brave the boat trip to Aird Bheag. In fact, she was to meet Ina there for the very first time, on 15th August 1935. The nurse was facing a serious dilemma as there were two expectant mothers in the Upper End. One of these was Katie Ann Macaulay of No.19 and the other was Jessie Macdonald out at Aird Bheag. On this day in particular she got word that she was needed to attend both the births but she couldn't be in two locations at the same time. The prediction had been that the Breanais baby would arrive first. However, in Aird Bheag the other baby had different ideas. There were also complications. The nurse had no real choice; it would have to be the dreaded boat trip. She attended the birth but things were far from straight forward and the surgeon had to be called. He was Mr. Jamieson who originally came from Shetland.

(If it had not been for the quick thinking of a fisherman from Steòrnabhagh this surgeon would never have practised medicine at all. As a boy, he had fallen into the harbour at Lerwick and was saved from drowning by this same fisherman who, incidentally he noticed, had a double thumb. The two were reunited in Steòrnabhagh hospital many years later when Mr. Jamieson noticed that the patient he was treating had a double thumb. He was able to introduce himself and to thank the fisherman for saving his life!)

Jessie's condition required a series of follow up visits by the nurse. As these visits were not emergencies the nurse chose the more strenuous method of reaching Aird Bheag. She cycled from Mangurstadh road-end to *Mol Linnis* and then took to the hills, walking by *Griomabhal* and then down *Gleann Sgaladail* where she was collected by boat. She would return on the same day by that route.

In 1947 there was another emergency call to Aird Bheag. Ina was only 12 years old and was doubled up with pain. This time Dr. Matheson arrived by boat and appendicitis was diagnosed so Ina had to be taken to hospital for surgery.

Nurse Macqueen was the first of the Upper End nurses to be appointed. She arrived in 1927 and stayed in the house built for her at Mangurstadh road-end. This nursing service was partly paid for by the West Coast Mission and partly by subscription from the people of the district. She was a resourceful, strong, and hardy woman who turned out whatever the weather. Even into the teeth of a gale she would pedal her bicycle to anyone who needed her help. She came from Staffin, An t-Eilean Sgitheanach, and always took her annual leave

124

there. Each time she returned she would complain that Uig was not as good as her home country. On one occasion Ina's grandfather, Donald *Taggaidh* Morrison of No.1 Mangurstadh, fed up listening to her moaning, told her in no uncertain terms that "*cha d'thainig duine no beathach a riamh a dh'Uig a dh'iarr às*" (no man or beast ever came to Uig, who wanted to leave it.)

In 1948, the Labour Government introduced the National Health Service, and the nurse got a car to replace the bicycle and the doctor no longer sent the dreaded bill after a visit. In 1953 the Macdonald family left Aird Bheag, much to the relief of the nurse who would never have to face that boat trip again. Nurse Macqueen retired in 1959, after 35 years of devoted service; she had served the Upper End of Uig well.

More stories of crofting life in Aird Bheag can be found in the memoir 'An Trusadh' by John MacDonald, Ina's brother. It was published in 2011 by The Islands Book Trust.

1936 - Macdonald Family in Aird Bheag
(L-R) John, Peggy, Jessie holding Ina,
Iain na h-Airde Bige and Christina

Late 1930s - Aird Bheag
Ina and her siblings
(L-R) John, Peggy, Ina and Christina

1950 - Iain na h-Airde Bige
& Jessie Macdonald, Aird Bheag

Aird Bheag in the 1950s

2006 - Dr Beveridge with her husband
and Iain and Ina in Mol Linnis

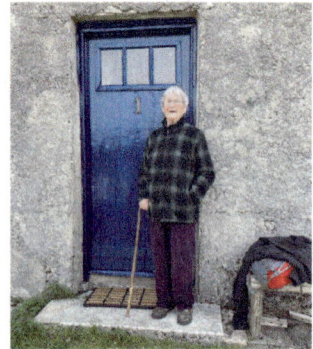

2021 - Ina Macdonald in Aird Bheag

AND OTHER STORIES...

More Falbh A' Chladach

At one time, beachcombing was an essential part of the crofting economy. The proof of this was plain to see when we recently renovated our house. Every other rafter, most of the floor joists, and the lintels, all showed the tell-tale signs of their origin. They came from the local builders' merchants, Flotsam & Jetsam Ltd located on the nearest beach, and at least a third of the volume of each timber had already been consumed by shipworm. Our stairs were quite eccentric, not a single tread or riser was the same width or height as the next! The strandline never provides exactly what you need but you could usually find something that would do or could be adapted. So, if you were building a house in the 1930s why waste the little money you had on new timber when the sea provided such a wealth and variety.

For some people beachcombing was not just a pastime, it was a way of life. They couldn't let a tide go by without checking to see what had been brought in. It was like a drug and there were quite a few 'addicts' in the Upper End. Like all the best addictions, part of the process was not totally legal. Officially things washed up on the beach are referred to as 'wreck'. Flotsam consists of goods lost from a ship in a storm or when it has sunk, and technically they remain the property of the original owner. Jetsam is deliberately thrown overboard to lighten the load and thus avoid sinking. Derelict is property abandoned at sea -just rubbish really, and lagan is cast overboard in such a way that it can be recovered later. Actually, it should all be reported to the Coastguard or Receiver of Wreck. Iain's father *Tobaidh* would visit the 'Excise' in Steòrnabhagh during the war years to pay for the timber that he found on the beach. It was charged at 1/- a plank and *Tobaidh* declared a dozen planks and duly paid his 12/- saying that this should cover it. The payment was a safeguard against inspection but no one ever came out to check which was just as well, as there were a lot more than twelve planks at No.1 Islibhig.

The variety of things that washed up is quite incredible, and unexpected. For example, in 1924, long before *The Politician* sank off Eirisgeigh, Malcolm *Saltier* Buchanan from Breanais, disappeared for three days. He was eventually discovered, sleeping soundly alongside a 40-gallon drum of extra strong whisky, down by the curing house. It should have been diluted at two or three to one, but *Saltier* hadn't bothered with that.

Another drum was washed up at Hùisinis opposite the village on An Sgarp and although it had been identified the *Scarpach*s had not got around to removing it from the beach. Someone had died on the island and an all-night wake was taking place. If the drum was not above high-water mark then it was fair game, so a clandestine expedition was mounted from Breanais. Donald *Tailleach* Macaulay of No.19, John *Seochan* Maclean of No.3, the Morrison brothers of No.20 (John *Scundar* and Norman *Block*) and Murdo Buchanan, rowed out at night to recover the whisky. As they neared An Sgarp the oars were wrapped in sacking to muffle the sound. When they landed they laid their jackets on the ground and rolled the drum over them, down to the waiting boat. Not just a drum of whisky went missing that night – five or so bannocks, newly cooked by *Seochan's* wife, also disappeared in the early hours. The contents of the newly acquired drum was rapidly transferred to any containers they could find, and hidden, but the empty drum was just left lying around. There were a few sore heads the next day but mainly the spirit was kept for weddings, funerals and for medicinal purposes. There is a suspicion to this day that not all the 1-gallon and 5-gallon stoneware jars were recovered and that some still lie buried somewhere. If you see a *bodach* furiously digging on the Breanais moor you can be sure it's not peat that he's after!

I heard about a *bodach* who found a drum that had come ashore. He had hoped to receive a finder's reward and so he reported it to the authorities. In due course an official arrived, struck the bung from the drum and the amber liquid poured out onto the ground until eventually all that was left was the delectable smell. The excise man got into his car and drove off. As the dust settled, the *bodach* could be seen staring at the damp patch, his head shaking in disbelief. His pockets were empty, for there was no reward.

Yet another drum is said to have washed up on Mangurstadh shore. Fearful of the contents (after all it could be poisonous), the *bodachs* decided to try it out on a very old *cailleach*, who was presumably expendable! She took a full tot, and promptly fell to the ground in a faint. They were aghast at what they had done – she was surely dead. Eventually she regained consciousness, declaring that it was a powerful dram and promptly took another. The *bodach*s were made of sterner stuff, and took quite a few before they all ended up in much the same condition as the *cailleach*!

Ma's breug bhuam e, is breug thugam e. (If it came false from me, it came false to me.)

I have never really considered beachcombing to be a particularly hazardous activity. Although on a few occasions I have found objects that once picked up and examined, have turned out to be potentially very dangerous. Such items are things like unfired flares or poisons in containers. It is only after you have picked them up, that you realise that you should have left them well alone. On these occasions it is only after the event that you realise how lucky you have been. One *Uigeach* was not so lucky.

It was in late November or early December 1919 that Murdo Macleod, *Murchadh Post* of An Cliobh was carrying out his usual search of the strandline on the beach close by his blackhouse. He was always on the lookout for useful items. On this occasion he found a small tin box that intrigued him, so he took it back home to give it a closer inspection. In the box were a number of steel or brass tubes. He hadn't a clue what they were but as the sea had obviously been at them, he considered them to be harmless. His son Angus was eager to see what his father had found and was standing close by. Murdo removed one of the tubes and raised it to examine it more closely. There was a sudden and unexpected explosion that badly damaged Murdo's left hand and his face. Pieces of metal flew everywhere. One fragment hit Angus in the leg. The metal tube was, in fact, a detonator for a mine or bomb. Luckily for the two, the District Nurse Miss Jeannie Maclean was on hand to dress their wounds and arrange for them to be transferred to Steòrnabhagh Hospital. Fortunately the boy was not badly hurt and was soon discharged but Murdo's wounds were far more severe. After two weeks he returned home but his hand was not healing and the sight in his left eye was affected. Jeannie Maclean changed his dressings on a regular basis and discovered two chunks of brass still lodged in his hand. She used all her skill and patience to remove these foreign objects, and soon his hand began to heal.

(Nurse Maclean was excellent at her job and rendered valuable service during the 'flu epidemic of 1918 and she had no maternity losses in the two years that she served Uig). Meanwhile, Murdo's sight remained a problem, and so he was sent to Glasgow for treatment. They soon discovered that his left eyeball had been punctured in three places and the only remedy was to remove his eye. He also had a piece of shattered and decaying bone extracted from his thumb. When he finally returned home in March 1920, they say his eyes looked quite normal. His great nephew, Iain *Tobaidh* knew his great uncle had a glass eye but until very recently he had not heard about the accident. This does seem strange because there was quite a lesson in the story for a young boy about what not to do with strange objects that you find on the sands.

Boxes seem to make a habit of being washed up on An Cliobh beach. It is where the *Ezra* ran aground in 1896 with a cargo of timber, which turned out to be useful in the church at *Baile na Cille* and numerous other buildings.

In the late 1940s, Norman *Bodlan* Mackay discovered a large box on the shore. To his amazement and delight, when he opened it he found it was stuffed with paper money. The notes were completely soaked by seawater and had strange oriental symbols all over them. His neighbour Murdina Maclennan remembers visiting the house and seeing piles of notes drying out on the mantle shelf. *Bodlan* was convinced that this time he had hit the jackpot, but he wasn't quite sure how rich he was. Murdina thinks that the money was Chinese. *Bodlan* had such plans. He definitely was going to build himself a beautiful new house. After that there would still be enough for a completely different lifestyle. Sadly, all his dreams evaporated when he discovered that his wad of notes was almost worthless.

The subject of beachcombing was first prompted by a photograph of Iain *Tobaidh* sitting on the beach at Mealastadh surrounded by heaps of beachcombed timber. This image was from *The Scotsman* newspaper, news of the bonanza of 'finished' timber that had washed ashore, mainly in the Upper End, had made the national press. No one informed us! But we were aware that something momentous was happening, because of all the frantic activity. An unbelievable number of cars with empty trailers came past our house and soon returned with enough timber on each, to build a four bed-roomed house! By the time we twigged that it was "for free" and there for the taking, most of it had gone. We did manage to find a few lengths ourselves over the next few days. When the reporters arrived the piles of jetsam had inexplicably disappeared, and everyone played dumb; except for one, of course! Hence the photograph.

Shiver me timbers, it's wood galore for the isles

27 March 1998 – The Scotsman article featuring Iain Tobaidh with his beachcombing haul of wood at Mealastadh

Seeds and a Bottle

Since the 1970s, beachcombing has gradually been losing its appeal, as plastic has become more popular. Although for one Breanais resident it was a full-time occupation until very recently. He actually found and brought home far more material from the shore than each tide brought in. The answer to this conundrum, his wife assured me, is that she regularly returned his 'treasures' to the beach when he wasn't looking!

An occasional find is a smooth, brown, heart shaped seed, variously called a sea bean, Molucca Nut or Mary's Nut. It is the seed of a Central American plant. In the past it was treasured as a good luck charm, especially useful to pregnant women to ensure safe delivery. These seeds have floated across the Atlantic, first in the Gulf Stream and then in the North Atlantic Drift. Another Caribbean seed that occasionally washes up is larger and is well known nowadays. However, a very young D.J.Macleod of Einacleit had never seen one before. He was in a boat off An Sgarp, with his grandfather and others. He was in the bow and was very excited when he spotted a large brown, spiky thing in the water. The crew swung the tiller desperately and prayed that they would not hit the stray mine they were sure was dead ahead. To everyone's relief they avoided contact and there was no explosion but they were amazed to see that the 'thing' wasn't dangerous at all: it was a coconut – the first one that D.J. had ever seen! He was promised some milk but not from the cow. When they returned to shore the husk was removed and the nut split open but to his great disappointment there was no milk at all.

These seeds have taken anything from six to eighteen months to travel the 2,500 miles but possibly some travel much further and take a lot longer. In 1992 a bottle, containing a note, was found on the beach at Mealastadh. It had come from an 11-year-old girl holidaying on Prince Edward Island in the Gulf of St. Lawrence. Seven years previously, she had thrown the bottle into the sea wondering if it would ever be found, and then had forgotten all about it. Seven years later, a couple on holiday from the south of England found the bottle and reported their find to the *Stornoway Gazette*. A reporter did some research and tracked down the girl who was by then a 19-year-old student at college in St. John's, Newfoundland. She was absolutely amazed but did remember writing the message and placing it in the bottle.

Planks, Wrecks and a Heroine

It must be recognised that all who venture on the sea do so with considerable bravery. Very few of them went sailing for pleasure. Locally, the sea was a highway, a food resource, and a workplace. Lewis people, from the first settlers and the Norse Vikings through to more recent seamen in the navy, have had a great affinity with the sea. With so many skilled seamen available it is no wonder that the area of the UK, which lost the highest percentage of servicemen in the two World Wars of the twentieth century, was the Western Isles.

When I was discussing with Iain *Tobaidh* the subject of things like timber being washed up, he mentioned in passing that his great, great (or more) grandfather on his mother's side, was particularly grateful for one special piece of wood. It was a plank, and without it this gentleman, called Duncan Buchanan, would never have seen old age! He and his plank came ashore at Mealastadh. It appears that he was the victim of a shipwreck and was saved from drowning by clinging to this precious length of timber. He recovered from his ordeal and settled in Mealastadh. His ruined house, *Taigh Dhonnchaidh*, can still be found just outside the north-east corner of the walled park. Strangely the house is built east-west and the door faces south, from where the worst of the weather comes. Perhaps this confirms the story, because only a stranger to the area would build a house with such an exposed entrance.

Duncan Buchanan was not the only person to be washed up on the beaches of the Upper End. During World War 2, lifeboats arrived in August 1940 and early in 1941. The first was a wooden boat with fourteen men from the crew of the cargo ship *Geraldine Mary*, which was torpedoed ten or twelve days before. Seeing sheep on Mealastadh Island they landed and pulled the boat onto the sandy beach. They could not find a single inhabitant or a house, but someone spotted a building to the north. With great difficulty, due to the soft sand, they launched the boat and landed again, at *Mol Forsgeo*. They were temporarily cared for in houses at Breanais before boarding *Sgail*'s bus to Steòrnabhagh. In appreciation of the kindness and care shown to the survivors, the Anchor Donaldson Line donated £60 to Breanais's nursing fund. About two or three weeks later a steel lifeboat, also with fourteen men, from the torpedoed oil tanker *S.S.Labrea*, came ashore at *Mol Linnis*. The crew were exhausted and needed guidance on where to make a safe landing. Fortunately, Calum Buchanan, his brother Iain and Norman Morrison, were working with the lambs and were on hand to help. The survivors were in a poor state being covered from head to foot in thick black oil. Attempts were made to clean them up with rags, margarine, and paraffin. Again, it was *Sgail's* bus that took them to Steòrnabhagh the next day.

Early in 1941, a fifteen-year-old Iain *Tobaidh* was earning himself a 'bob', cycling to Mangurstadh to deliver a telegram to Malcolm Buchanan. It was good news for a change. An extra day's leave before he had to re-join the *Dunnotter Castle*, a converted passenger liner on convoy duty. At least eight of the crew of this boat were from Uig, five from Breanais and one each from Mangurstadh, Eadar Dhà Fhadhail and Cradhlastadh. As Iain took the shortcut across the sands, he noticed the Mangurstadh people pulling up an empty lifeboat. It was assumed that any survivors who had been in the boat, had already been rescued. Malcolm John Macritchie of No.10 Eadar Dhà Fhadhail , later purchased this boat from the customs.

Forty-three years earlier, a sailing boat was driven ashore on Mangurstadh sands. She was an eighty-eight ton Danish schooner, the *Grana* from Copenhagen, sailing from Iceland with a cargo of dried fish and was bound for Liverpool. Off the Faroe Islands they were hit by a bad north-easterly gale that smashed both the bow and stern, ripping the sails to shreds and twisting the hull so severely that she sprang a leak. The cargo had shifted and for four days they were at the mercy of the wind and the waves. Eventually they spotted Mangurstadh Sands and after scraping against some rocks, they were miraculously taken on a large wave, onto the sands. At this Point the story takes two forms. The *Highland News* states that the exhausted crew waited until low water to get ashore then made their way to the farmhouse. However, the other version, which was published in the *Strand Magazine* of 1897, says that the exhausted crew were amazed to see a woman, who at first, they took to be an angel, coming to their rescue. She was in fact Mrs. Christina Mackay, wife of the farmer, Mr. Donald Mackay, who was away in Steòrnabhagh on business, at the time. According to the magazine she:

actually saved, almost single-handed, the whole crew of the ship...She went heroically into the storm with her young son. Her gallant exertions resulted in the establishment of communication with the ship, by means of which the whole crew were saved from certain death...She then took the men into her own house and cared for them with almost maternal tenderness, nursing them for several days.

The local story describes the farmer's wife wading into the wild seas with a rope and then helping the crew to haul the anchor lines ashore. It was only her bravery and quick response that saved the entire crew. In recognition of her gallant and humane action, the Danish Government later presented her with a suitably inscribed clock. The cargo of about forty tons of dried cod and haddock and the hull of the ship were auctioned on the sands on Wednesday 4th November 1896. Timbers from this boat were used in the construction of the roof of the old whitehouse at No.1 Islibhig, and the ship's anchor chain and other bits of wreckage can occasionally be seen on the beach.

In the nineteenth century four wrecks were recorded at the Upper End. These were: the *Julia*, a brig from Sunderland carrying timber that came ashore, bottom up, at Mealastadh in October 1845; an unknown brig came ashore on the west side of

An Sgarp and later in Reàsort, as wreckage, in February 1850; the *Mazeppa*, another wooden brig, registered in Liverpool, was wrecked at Mealastadh in January 1854 and five years later a brig carrying cotton and oil was wrecked on An Sgarp.

Probably the saddest wreck in the south end of Uig occurred in 1932 and has already been referred to earlier. On the 12th March the *Fair Maid*, also known as *Margaret*, a nine year old, locally built boat with a lugsail, set off with another boat to lift lobster creels. She was last seen sailing to the west side of Eilean Mealastadh and disappeared behind a headland. The skipper was Cain Mackinnon whose father had been drowned some years earlier whilst rock fishing. In the crew was Cain's son Angus, John Buchanan, and a barely twenty-year-old Malcolm Macritchie. The day was fine, but an unexpected squall blew up and presumably the boat was driven onto rocks and destroyed. The bodies of the four men were never recovered.

A Kidnap and Two Rescues

Uig Bay was named by the Norse as a safe haven, which to the experienced sailor it may be, but many others have mistakenly relied on it for shelter in a storm. In the southeast corner of the bay, around both Carnais and Cradhlastadh are some treacherous rocks; many of them are submerged at high tides. In the spring of 1874, a beautiful fully rigged ship let down her anchor in the *Poll Gorm*, the worst anchorage in *Camus Uig*. She was the *La Marie de Dunquerque,* a French boat taking supplies to French fishermen stationed in Iceland. The people of Cradhlastadh warned them of the dangers as best they could but before the boat was moved to a safer spot it had dragged its anchor and become wedged in rocks just off *Triagh a' Chidhe*, Carnais. It was holed below the waterline, and the sea was pouring in. It was decided that the Cradhlastadh boats would ferry off the cargo and the ship would be refloated at high tide, and beached at Port Charnis for repair. While the work was carried out the French sailors, with their cargo of provisions, fishing tackle, lines and ropes, and much brandy and wine, were made very welcome in the village of Cradhlastadh.

In all, the Frenchmen's stay lasted six weeks, but not without incident. Whether it was out of boredom, lust or true love no one will ever know, but just as the boat was ready to depart, Annie Ruaridh, a 14-year-old Cradhlastadh beauty, was captured by the biggest and strongest of the French crew. Despite the entreaties of her family (her mother was a widow), and the rest of his shipmates, he would not release his embrace. It was her uncle George Macleod, the shoemaker, and his apprentice Donald Macdonald, who saved the day. With the help of a band of young village men, who by various elaborate means attempted to distract the kidnapper, Donald was able to wrench Annie free. Fortunately she was not injured in the incident. The

Frenchman returned to the ship in disgrace and without his chosen prize. As the repairs were complete, they were able to sail away immediately, not to Iceland as instructed, but home to France. Here, the captain and his mate were punished for dereliction of duty and disobeying orders. After all, little thought had been given to the poor fishermen in Iceland whose food, equipment and alcohol had all been consumed by the lucky Cradhlastadh folk! As for the love-lorn sailor, there was no punishment, just the scorn and ridicule of the other crew members. No one knows how the incident affected Annie because she never spoke of it. She was later married, but not to the gallant shoemaker's apprentice. She had children and enjoyed a long life, dying at the age of 89yrs. She was born Annie Macdonald, and one of her grandsons was Donald *Dolol* Macdonald of No.4 Cradhlastadh. The apprentice shoemaker Donald Macdonald, who played such an important role in the rescue, also married and one of his granddaughters was Peggy Ann Macdonald of Geisiadar. The story was completed in 1949 when another *Dolol*, the grandson of the rescued maiden, married Peggy Ann, the granddaughter of her rescuer.

As I have already mentioned, Uig Bay presents many hazards to boats entering it for the first time. Sixty-six years after the departure of the French ship, Cradhlastadh again played host to another boatload of sailors. It was a very hot day in the summer of 1940 when *Dolol*, his father John and Malcolm Macdonald of No.2 Cradhlastadh, were walking to the peats that were close to the Aird road. Suddenly one of them spotted a small boat on the horizon. Calum realised that the crew would inevitably steer towards *Sheilibhig Mhor* and the rocks. What a disaster, having survived the sinking of their ship, they were now about to drown within sight of safety! It was on the 7th June 1940 that the cargo ship of the Stanhope Line had been attacked. A U-boat had surfaced and used its gun to sink the Fleetwood bound *Stancor*, with its cargo of Icelandic fish. The crew had first been warned to take to their lifeboats before the attack commenced. The incident occurred 80 miles northwest of the Butt. Now two days later the exhausted survivors were in mortal danger. But not if Calum could prevent it! He was an educated man and always carried paper and a pencil with him. His quick thinking meant that he was already devising a rescue plan. Cycling up the An Aird road was Peter Angus Maclean from Timsgearraidh, the postman. Calum wrote instructions on a piece of paper and told Peter to give the message to the first person he saw. There were four people in An Aird with the job of watching the sea for anything unusual. One of them was *Calum Og*, Malcolm Matheson. He set off immediately to a Point where he could see the boat and communicate with them. With much shouting and waving of arms he persuaded the men in the lifeboat to steer further out into Uig Bay and come around Tolm to Cradhlastadh harbour, and to safety.

As soon as they were on dry land they wanted to telephone the authorities, notifying them of their survival. One of the men strode off across the *Traigh Mhor* to the telephone at No.8 Timsgerraidh. He wore a long thick greatcoat, which amazed everyone who saw him. Peggy Ann, who was hoeing potatoes with her father in Timsgerraidh remembers well seeing him in his coat and wondering how he could stand the heat in such a garment. The crew were taken to Steòrnabhagh. Their lifeboat, which was a wooden one and in good condition, found its way in due course to *Loch Suaineabhal*. For years it was used to ferry crofters to the fank and sheilings at the far end of the loch and back. The old boat was in poor condition and this new one came not a moment too soon.

FURTHER READING

Compulsory Education

I have been wading through the School Logbooks for the five Uig schools. Most of these still survive, many dating back to 1879, and are to be found in Stornoway Library. Since the first compulsory schools opened, the Head Teacher at each school was required to keep a record of school business on a weekly basis. The entries included visits by officials such as the Compulsory Officer, Chairman of the School Board, His/Her Majesty's Inspector of Schools, medical officers and nurses, peripatetic teachers, and others. Illnesses were recorded and so were school closures associated with infectious diseases. The seasonal activities on the crofts in the various townships were very well documented because apart from illness, these were the main reasons cited by pupils for not attending school.

In the early days, and right up to the 1960s, it seems that there was a constant battle between the authorities and the parents to ensure that all children attended school. Although most parents accepted the necessity for their children to receive an education, they also needed them to carry out essential activities on the croft. In fact, much of the seasonal work could not be adequately performed without a workforce consisting of adults and children. The Government required children to attend school whenever it was officially open. The Education Act Scotland 1872 had introduced compulsory education for all children between the ages of 5 and 13 years. Each School Board was required to appoint a Compulsory Officer, to be paid £3 per annum, whose job it was to check on attendance and to question the parents about their children's absences. If pupils did not attend regularly then parents were summonsed to appear before the School Board. If they still persisted in allowing their children to absent themselves from school, the parents would be prosecuted and could be fined or even imprisoned. In one School Log, the head teacher states that neither the School Board nor the parents care much about attendance. Another suggests that most of the excuses given for non-attendance were trivial and even dishonest – children who were supposed to be ill were to be seen running around their township or fetching peats some miles from home!

In the early years of compulsory education (1880s and 1890s), there were reports that children, especially the younger ones, often did not appear in school when there was frost and snow – but sometimes they did! The Headmaster of Islibhig School wrote on the 20th of February 1885:

The whole week was extremely cold with snow, frost and a piercing wind. Attendance as a consequence is reduced, but seeing young children coming bare foot over snow and frost, from a distance, as some of them have done this week, is gratifying in a sense but rather unpleasant in another.

Weather conditions were cited as the reason for poor attendance from the 1880s right up to the 1970s. Snow blocked roads a few times each winter. Severe gales and driving rain were also mentioned, as well as thin and scanty clothing! On occasions many of the children would arrive at school literally soaked to the skin. Rather than have them take chills, they would be sent back home.

At first it appears that there were no official set school holidays. Children could be found in school on Christmas Day, New Year's Day and even on Saturdays. In Breanais in the 1880s, they did get 12th January off school to celebrate the Old New Year! They also got holidays for the Communion Fast Days and Harvest Thanksgiving Day. It was up to the Head Teacher and School Board, to decide when to close the school, but there were a minimum number of sessions to be completed. The school holidays were usually precipitated by the lack of children at their desks, especially the older ones. This occurred at various times of the year, coinciding with the seasonal work on the croft. In April and May up to four weeks were given, for ploughing, planting and peat cutting. In June and July, cattle were driven to and from the sheilings, and sheep were sheared. In August many children were absent for heather pulling when: "the finest and longest kind is used for making ropes which secure the thatch upon the houses." In September there would be another four-week break given for harvesting. At very low spring tides, the children would be on the seashore gathering winkles and whelks or cutting seaweed. However, these holidays could not be too long, as a proportion of a teacher's pay was calculated according to pupil attendance.

One particular Headmaster was absent himself on several occasions because he was required to attend the Sheriff's Court in Steòrnabhagh. He was called as a witness for the prosecution of parents who persistently failed to ensure that their children attend school. Excuses for absence that were deemed inadequate included weather, nursing, messages, sheep shearing, house thatching, want of shoes, rebuilding walls, wind too strong, not well clad, gathering lambs and cleaning drains! It was not until 1928 that school holidays were fixed and coordinated throughout the district. It was then required that parents got permission in advance for their children to be absent for croft work, although this did not seem to be very vigorously enforced. During the period of the Second World War the regulation was relaxed.

There were many occasions when parents of a township got together and jointly refused to send their children to school. These were recorded in the Logbooks as 'parent strikes'. The Aird children were kept away from school for a period of time, until the parents were promised an adequate path across the moor. Many of their children, especially the girls, suffered from badly cut feet in the summer; in the winter the moor became impossibly boggy. The parents of Cradhlastadh withheld their children until they were promised a road that would save the pupils from their dependency on the tides. On another occasion these same parents went on strike until the butting stirk on the Manse Glebe was adequately controlled! The children were so terrified of the wild beast that they would not cross the Glebeland. There was also a parent strike in Bhaltos because of the failure to appoint a new Head Teacher, a strike at Riof to push for a path, and the provision of a bridge to Bhaltos School.

There were some holidays that were 'sprung' upon the schools from officials' sources. On 22nd June 1897 there was a day's holiday for Queen Victoria's Diamond Jubilee. In early 1900 there was a half-day off to celebrate the relief of Ladysmith, Natal, South Africa. In 1909 Lord Pentland, Secretary of State for Scotland, and his wife visited Bhaltos School and asked that the pupils be given a half day. On 18th August 1919, the King granted all schools a week's holiday for the Peace Celebrations. In the 1920s there were days off for two Royal weddings; one was Princess Mary and other the Duke of York. In 1927 there was a holiday granted as a mark of respect for the funeral in Steòrnabhagh of Dr. Iain Robertson, Chief HMI of Schools for Scotland. Mr. T.B. Macaulay of Sun Life Canada visited Uig in June 1929 and all the children were given the day off for the festivities. In the 1930s there were holidays for the weddings of the Duke of Kent and Gloucester, the funeral of George V and the coronation of George VI.

The Silver Jubilee in 1935 did not bring a day off for the pupils of Islibhig School but there was a much better celebration. Miss Matheson hired a horse and cart to take everything for a picnic down to Mealastadh sands. There were flags and bunting, games and jelly, jam buns and

145

sweets. Everyone got a present; gold painted bowls and jugs with bluebirds on, and whistles and toy cars. The sun shone and it wasn't like school at all!

A whole week was given for the outbreak of the Second World War in 1939, but only one day for VE Day in 1945. In 1947 there was a holiday for the wedding of Princess Elizabeth. When her father died in 1952 some schools took a half day for his funeral, while others just held a two-minute silence. In May 1953 a holiday of three days was granted for the coronation of Queen Elizabeth. Two more holidays were allowed for the birth of Prince Charles and another for Princess Margaret's wedding. In June 1965 there was another holiday to celebrate Magna Carta Day. In the 1970s days off were permitted for the Queen's 25th wedding anniversary and later her Silver Jubilee.

1935 - Islibhig School Jubilee Celebrations in Mealastadh

Diseases

The Log Books of the five Uig Schools revealed a lot about Uig life from 1879 until the immediately post-war period. The agricultural year was covered very well – as a series of seasonal absences, with excuses given to the Compulsory Officer. These were recorded, often with comments and sometimes interesting details of crofting practice. The severest weather was well recorded and included snow blocking roads, gale force winds, torrential and persistent rain. Besides preventing some or all of the children from attending school these conditions also caused roof and window leaks, blowdowns causing schoolrooms to fill with smoke and floor flooding. However, by far the most interesting and disturbing reflection of Uig life recorded in the Logbooks were the entries regarding school closures or pupil exclusion due to illness.

The illnesses mentioned in the Logbooks will be familiar to the older residents of Uig but are almost unheard of in the present school. The most feared disease was probably measles. It was highly infectious and was spread by coughs and sneezes. The patient would suffer a high temperature and rash, but the complications often had very serious consequences leading to pneumonia, ear and eye problems, brain damage and even death. Even today there are a million deaths worldwide each year. Whooping cough was another feared childhood illness. Hacking coughing fits would last until there was no air left in the lungs, and then there was a sharp intake of breath causing the 'whoop'. The child could have up to fifteen of these fits in a day, and it could go on for twelve weeks. Bronchitis, pneumonia, and death were not uncommon. Mumps was also a problem. The symptoms often appeared three weeks after infection, and it could lead to deafness and sometimes fatal meningitis.

Scarlet fever was another common childhood illness; it was caused by a streptococcal bacterium. The main symptom was a rash on the tongue, known by everyone as strawberry tongue, but complications such as rheumatic fever could lead to heart damage, pneumonia, and death. Tuberculosis occurred but was rarely recorded in the Logbooks, however typhoid fever was. This salmonella bacterium came from contaminated water and was extremely virulent. The whole family usually suffered from headaches, peritonitis and sometimes kidney failure – it was often fatal.

Another childhood horror struck in 1938, just before the outbreak of war. Children in Lochcroistean School began to suffer from sore throats and developed high temperatures. One of the pupils was suspected of having Diphtheria, but the authorities felt that it was an isolated case. However, in December poor Kirsty Macdonald of 11, Geisiadar died, and she was only seven years old. The school was immediately fumigated, and swabs were taken from pupils in mid-January. For some unknown reason these proved to be negative for Diphtheria and despite parental protests the authorities were convinced that there was no need to panic. A second set of swabs was taken in March and these tested positive. Suddenly everything had changed, and all the Uig schoolchildren were immunised but by then another two children were dead. Not all child deaths were recorded in the School Logbooks. However, during the fifty-year period 1892 to 1942 I found references to twenty-three children of school age dying and I am sure there were many more.

Each outbreak of infection prompted the medical authorities to issue a certificate to the child, an exclusion order to the parents and a closure notice to the school concerned. Pupils who had suffered an illness would need a certificate to return to school and often their house had to be fumigated. This required the family to burn a sulphur candle. The candles were made in Germany and came in tins. Some wry wit referred to them as German gas – presumably a reference back to First World War trench warfare. You had to vacate the house for three or four hours while the candle burned, and the smoke did its work. When you eventually got back into your home everything smelled of sulphur, and this lasted for some days. Your clothes stank of it for weeks! The same process was also required for the schoolroom. The teacher at Lochcroistean complained in the Logbook that she nearly burned down the school premises. She placed the candle as instructed on a plate, put this on a bench, lit it and retired. When she returned, she discovered a cracked plate and a severely scorched bench.

The outbreak of an infectious disease usually led to the temporary closure of a school, sometimes lasting a week or two, but occasionally much longer. On 8th November 1918 Cradhlastadh School was closed and, apart from a few days in late January, did not reopen until 17th March 1919.

The worst pandemic of a deadly strain of influenza was gripping the world. The illness is thought to have started early in 1918 amongst the soldiers living and fighting in the wretchedly squalid conditions of the trenches in France. Both sides in the conflict suffered, but not enough to bring the war to an end. However, as the soldiers began returning home, the bacterium mutated and became more virulent. Very soon it had spread to the four corners of the globe. Despite its remoteness, Uig was not to be exempted from the full horrors of the illness. During three weeks in November six Uigeachs died; including a four-year-old, two 15-year-olds and two young men just 18 and 19. One Bhaltos family was particularly badly hit. On Saturday 16th November, Mrs. Smith's husband Donald died, and on the following Monday her son Donald also succumbed. In the Stornoway Gazette it was reported that, "the double funeral from Mrs. Smith's house took place. It was a most pathetic and impressive spectacle witnessing the two coffins being taken out and carried in the same procession to the local cemetery, and laid side by side in the same grave". This disease went on to kill many millions of people worldwide – far more than died in the First World War. After a closure of twenty weeks Cradhlastadh School re-admitted pupils, but by early July it was again closed due to an outbreak of measles. On 1st September, the school opened its doors for the new academic year. During the previous year it had been closed due to illness for twenty-seven weeks.

Authorities ordered the closure of a school whenever an outbreak of an infectious disease affected any of the children attending the school, or their families. Sometimes rumours of illness spread around the district and parents panicked. Children were withheld from attending school until reassurance was provided and even then some would not take the risk. School closure probably did help to reduce the spread of contagion but, by the time these diseases had been diagnosed by a doctor, many of the pupils in a school would already have been infected. Until the 1930s, apart from home remedies and the tireless efforts of the district nurses, there was little that could be done to cure these illnesses. It was normal just to keep the child at home and pray. Parents were reluctant to call or visit the doctor. They knew that he was probably no more effective than the nurse and they would eventually receive an unaffordable bill for his services, and his travel. An example of this situation occurred in 1937 when the four Macdonald children in Islibhig all went down with scarlet fever. The nurse attended but she recommended that they call the doctor. He made two visits, and later sent them a bill for £2-18-6. Angus Macdonald, their father had been working for the council on road repairs but his six months was up and he had been forced to relinquish the job and return to the dole. This was the way things were in those days. The unemployed spent half the year on the dole, and the other half they were given a paid job. His weekly dole at that time was less than the doctor's bill. It is no wonder people were so reluctant to call the doctor. As a comparison with today's prices you could buy a packet of twenty cigarettes or a gallon of petrol for 1/- a brand new 'Flying Dragon' bicycle for £3 from J.D.Williams, or a second hand one from Peter Macritchie of Eadar Dhà Fhadhail for £2-10-0. You would repay him when you could afford it!

From the mid-1930s onwards, greater efforts were being made to improve children's health. The district nurse made regular visits to schools to check the children and advise on hygiene. The Medical Officer also made an annual visit to every school. I am told by a reliable source that this event was eagerly anticipated by some of the older boys. There was a thorough health check made of every pupil. This took place in the classroom and was therefore in full view of everyone. When the doctor used his stethoscope to listen to their heart, the girls were asked to lift their blouses. At that moment the doctor was not the only one carrying out a chest examination! Even though it was a very interesting subject to the senior boys, female anatomy was not on the curriculum.

After the Second World War the doctor and the medicines he prescribed became free. An inoculation programme was put in place, and this changed the outlook for the health of school aged children tremendously. Whether it would have had any real effect or not, the HMI in the 1920s attempted to stamp out a 'filthy habit' which could have been responsible for the spread of infectious diseases. He ordered that the 'disgusting and unhygienic' practice of cleaning a slate by spitting on it was to be stopped immediately. However, on subsequent visits, he had to admit that despite his ruling the practice still persisted! It was not spitting on slates that was responsible for the high incidence of illness amongst the children. The contributory factors that led to the high child mortality rate at the time, were the scarcity of effective drugs, poor nutrition, inadequate clothing, and the lack of proper footwear in winter. The latter two of these got a significant amount of coverage in the School Logbooks.

It was interesting to read about recent events at Uig School, where pupils came to school in fancy dress or pyjamas, to raise money for children less fortunate than themselves. In the early part of the twentieth century Head Teachers were recording events that show that children here in Uig, were being regarded as deserving of other people's charity. Bundles of clothes and clogs were distributed in one school, while biscuits and syrup from The Glasgow Relief Committee were provided in another. Sporting tenants of Uig Lodge were often sending fruit and cake to local schools or providing tea parties at the Lodge. An American school collected toys, and these were given to the children in one school. Probably the most poignant of the stories about the receipt of charity was not recorded in any Logbook, but is still etched on the memory of Finlay Maciver, Cairisiadar. A consignment of wellington boots arrived at Lochcroistean School, but not enough for everyone. Young Finlay was successful in the draw and was promised a pair. For days he dreamed about jumping in puddles without getting his feet wet. On the day of the great distribution there was a change in the arrangements. It transpired that there was a more deserving case. A rather sickly little girl who had very inadequate footwear was to get the boots that had been promised to him. He understood the argument, accepted the outcome but he never quite came to terms with the pain of seeing, on a daily basis, 'his' wellies on the feet of another child! Incidentally Finlay turned out not to be as immune from illness as his teacher thought. In the 1938 diphtheria outbreak at Lochcroistean school, Finlay himself was one of the victims. Fortunately for him, Dr. Maclennan was insistent that his parents send him to the 'Fever Hospital' in Steornabhagh where he was diagnosed with the illness, and subsequently treated. Had he stayed at home he may well have died.

From the opening of the new Uig School on 20th December 1971 to the present day it was heartening to read that the worst illness recorded was a bout of vomiting and diarrhoea in 1992, and the occasional outbreak of head lice, but nothing more serious. There is no doubt that the National Health Service, the development of vaccination and antibiotics, as well as housing grants, unemployment benefit etc. have transformed children's health in the last sixty years. Many of the diseases mentioned in this article have almost been eradicated from the British Isles. Conditions in school and at home; in fact, life in general for children in Uig is very different nowadays.

Harris Tweed in Uig

The Harris Tweed industry, according to the traditional story, is said to have begun in the mid-19th century. The two Macleod sisters, originally from Pabbay in the Sound of Harris, were living in a blackhouse in Strond and producing tweeds on their looms. The story is that these were the first tweeds to be called Harris Tweeds and were woven in Murray tartan for the workers on the Dunmore Estate, Harris. After the death of Lord Dunmore in the early 1840s, his widow took over the running of the estate. She was very interested in the tweeds made by Harris crofters and decided to help in the improvement of the product and its marketing. In Lewis, the idea of producing cloth to sell rather than just for home use, caught on first in the Lochs district, and then in Uig. Before 1920, Uig and Lochs were reputedly the centres of weaving in Lewis. Around about 1900, the Scottish Home Industries Association, with money from the Congested District Board, had set up a depot in Uig, where weavers could deliver their finished tweeds.

In those early days it was the beart mhòr (handloom) that was used to produce the tweeds. The shuttle was large and had wheels on the underside and back, and it was propelled across the warp by a sharp pull on a handle. This was known as the 'flying shuttle'. In Bhaltos there were at least five, they were owned by: Donald Maclean No.10, Malcolm Mackay No.7, Donald Macleod No.29, and Donald Maclennan No.11, and Calum Iain Maclennan at No.38 An Cliof. In the Upper End there was a beart mhòr at No.1 Breanais (Finlay Maclean), at No.11 Breanais (Malcolm Buchanan) and at No.8 Islibhig (John Macaulay). This large loom was a great improvement on the even earlier beart bheag, which was a small loom that employed a sheep's shinbone as a shuttle. This was thrown across the width of the loom through the shed in the warp threads. It was mainly the women who used the beart bheag, and the men who used the beart mhòr. In the very early days, all the processes were carried out on the croft. The wool was sheared from the sheep, washed and dyed, carded and then spun on a spinning wheel, before being woven into cloth. Much of the cloth made on the small looms was for the crofters' own use, but enough could be produced on the large looms to sell or barter.

In the early years of the twentieth century there were a few carding mills on the island, which helped speed up the production of yarn. Sir Samuel Scott built a water-powered carding mill near Tarbert in 1900. Not long after there were mills in Steòrnabhagh. In 1903 Aeneas Mackenzie bought the defunct Patent Slip, which had been built by Sir James Matheson for building and repairing ships. He erected a carding mill on the site. In 1906 the first spinning machines were installed in mills in Steòrnabhagh. Kenneth Mackenzie Ltd. had a spinning mill on Lewis Street. The trademark of the company used the image of Norman Smith of No.2, Ungesiadar, weaving on the beart mhòr.

It was now possible for a weaver to take his own wool to be carded and spun for him at the mill. There was talk of a spinning mill in Uig, but the closest was built in Siabost in 1915. There were meetings to complain about this in Uig, and talks with the weavers in Lochs, but to no avail. There is a story of a Breanais weaver taking his sheared wool over the moor to Tarbert and returning with yarn the same day.

There were some merchants who provided the yarn for the weavers, and the finished pieces of cloth were often bartered for ready-made clothing, groceries and so on. In the 1920s, weavers purchased meat from Sammy Newall, one of the Steòrnabhagh butchers, and paid him with lengths of tweed. He accumulated so much tweed that he was forced to sell it on the mainland. This prompted him to buy the empty Patent Slip Mill in Steòrnabhagh, and start producing yarn, and then finishing the woven cloth himself. He kept his butcher business going and paid the weavers with meat. Eventually his tweed business was going so well, that after 1923 he was able to pay weavers in real money. However, at Siabost mill, the system of bartering went on well into the 1930s.

Most of the old handlooms were abandoned in the early 1920s or before, for the very good reason that there was precious little money to be made. An Uig correspondent to the *Stornoway Gazette* writing in November 1921 stated that:

Tweed-making, the principal industry here for many years past, is a failure. Prices for tweeds are so low that it is a waste of time and labour to bother making them at all.

However, there were a few of the old looms being used much later. In Islibhig, the Rev. Alec Maclennan, the Free Presbyterian Missionary who lived in the Missionary's house from 1947 to 1949, was using the old beart mhòr to

156

weave blankets. He would produce two blankets that were then sewn together to make a cover large enough for a bed.

After the First World War there were ex-servicemen who had lost a hand, and one of the reasons for introducing the Hattersley domestic semi-automatic treadle powered loom to the island, was to give them an opportunity to make a living for themselves. Presumably, despite the sacrifices they had made for their country, compensation and an adequate pension were out of the question. Originally designed for the Balkans, Turkey and Greece, these looms eventually caught on for everyone in Lewis and Harris, because of the superior speed of cloth production and the more intricate patterns they could weave. Lord Leverhulme's interest in the industry, coupled with the serious decline of the herring fishery and the poor price of cured fish from the long line fishery, meant that weaving became a much more important part of the island economy. He had great plans to build weaving sheds close to townships to house many Hattersley looms. The weavers would be employed from nine to five, six days a week, weaving tweed for a wage. However, this arrangement did not suit crofter-weavers, who would only weave when the croft work allowed, and the idea was eventually dropped.

Hugh Mackay, Carisiadar, bought the very first Hattersley loom in Uig, it was a single shuttle model. He was a marine engineer, trained in Glasgow, and could strip down the loom and reassemble it without difficulty. If he had a problem, he had no one locally to ask for advice, so he would get on his motorbike and go to Steòrnabhagh. However, he admitted that quite often he had forgotten the solution, by the time he got back home! In 1936, John Buchanan of No7, Bhaltos, organised a meeting at Bhaltos school for local people. Pat Skinner from Kenneth Mackenzie Ltd was there and they arranged for Alasdair Hare from Lochs (*mac puithair Tharmoid Doinn*), known as '*am breabadair*', to

157

stay in the village for a few weeks. He went from shed-to-shed teaching as he went.

The Hattersley loom was extremely well made and very robust. It could be left for months or even years, as long as the sliders were regularly oiled, it could be used straight away. There was no fear of rust seizing up the machinery. It rarely broke down, but if there was a problem spares could be purchased from the agents, the Crofters or Stephen Burns. It was a compact loom that could be easily fitted into a domestic setting, but as a result the width of the cloth produced was only 29 inches. This has caused problems for the tailoring industry, which has repeatedly demanded a wider fabric. Some years ago a new loom was developed by Bonas Griffith Ltd, Sunderland, that could produce a double width tweed. Some saw this as the answer to the decline in the industry. However, those that bought these new looms had serious problems. The demand for Harris Tweed had not really improved, and although there were grants available to help with buying a new loom, there was no scheme whereby the balance of the cost would be deducted, only when money was being earned. So, whether there was a tweed to weave or not, the bank still demanded repayment of the loan. The older weavers were very suspicious that demand for single width would fall when the new looms appeared. No one in Uig converted to the double width.

It seems that fashion has been the real driver of demand in the last few years. There was once a time where an item of clothing that lasted a lifetime was a very desirable thing. In the 1930s Harris Tweed was the preferred dress for hunting, fishing, shooting, and even for attempting to climb Everest. At its peak, in the late 1960s the industry employed 2,500 people, produced 7 million metres of cloth per annum, and had a turnover of £20 million a year. In the 1970s the heroes in numerous Holywood blockbuster films wore Harris Tweed jackets. How things have changed, nowadays people buy clothes that within a few months have gone out of fashion, are thrown away or taken to the charity shop. In the first few years of the 21st century, there was a 60% decline in the industry. There was also a time when Harris Tweed was used for bus and railway carriage seats, but now it is all synthetic fibres.

Suddenly in mid-2004 there were tweeds to be woven, at very short notice – Nike had decided to sell trainers made of Harris Tweed. They ordered 9,550 metres of two by two Russian twill, a pattern designed by D.J. Mackay, of Luskentyre. Forty weavers produced the necessary amount in ten weeks. The shoes eventually went on sale in October 2004. The BBC 2 screened a programme about Harris Tweed, and Vogue Magazine featured the cloth and the industry. The shoes sold well, and Nike ordered more Harris Tweed for hooded-tops. But for the single width weavers, things were very slow, and the Hattersley looms largely remained idle. In 1959 there were 54 full-time weavers in Uig. That was a third of the labour force earning their living at the loom. In 2005 only one person described himself as a weaver, all the rest were retired or ex-weavers.

Weaving was once regarded by many as a good way to earn a living. You could start and finish work when you saw fit. The job could be fitted conveniently into the crofting year. True there were times when the demand was heavy and other jobs had to be left undone – but the money was good! If there was a constant demand there was no problem, but there was a drawback, you were self-employed, not an employee of the mill. Therefore, when things were slack there was no dole – you had to rely on 'the social'. There was never really a seasonal difference, but just before the mill holiday period (mid July to mid August) there were extra tweeds. After the holiday things were often very slack. Eventually the Union negotiated holiday money while the mill was closed. At one time the weavers that lived closer to

Steornabhagh got tweeds in slack times, whereas none would find their way into the remoter areas. The Weaver's Union, a branch of the Transport and General Workers Union, thrashed out a new system of distribution, so that weavers in the most distant areas from the mill got their fair share.

Nowadays, the Hattersley loom is a museum exhibit, not a good way of making a living. Even a double-width loom could be risky. Although the vast majority of Harris Tweed is now double-width, some have managed to work independently of the mills and have marketed their tweeds themselves. One such is Breanais Tweed, which was Ian Sutherland's business, which he started when he was living in Breanais. He continued to weave and trade for some years, from his new home in Mealbost, but then decided to call it a day. This business was bought and relocated to NIs and produces tweeds that are not necessarily Harris tweeds. Another independent weaver, still very much in business is A.J. Mackay of Luskentyre, who took the original Nike order, and has more orders in the pipeline. It would be sad to see the end of this industry but the prospects are not very good. In 2005 there were few working looms in Uig. The last Hattersley woven Uig tweed, was produced at No.1, Islibhig

WW1: Internment in Holland

Some years ago, John Macdonald, Islibhig, told me an intriguing story about when his father was held 'prisoner' in Holland during the First World War and how he had come home on leave, at least twice. Even more amazing was that these internees all returned dutifully to Holland each time, resisting the temptation to stay at home!

I duly noted the story, but forgot about it until early in 2005, when I saw a letter in the Stornoway Gazette asking for information about Lewismen interned at Groningen, Holland from 1914-1918. John told me that he had responded to the letter. I decided to do some research myself about other Uigeachs who had been interned. There turned out to be twenty men involved in the events that occurred in the early months of the First World War. Twelve of them were interned, another five were taken prisoner and three escaped altogether. However, it was very difficult to get any details about what actually happened. None of those I asked could give me much information. The men had apparently spoken very little about their time in Holland. In contrast, the information from Holland was very good. Residents of Groningen had taken a great interest in the sailors, who were shut up in what they called the 'Engelse Kamp', and what the internees called HMS Timbertown.

Disaster in Antwerp

Apparently in about 1909, a Committee decided that some money needed to be injected into the Uig economy. Until then there was so little actual money around that the residents were unable to pay their dues for the nursing service in the district. It was proposed that men in the remoter areas would be allowed to join the Royal Naval Reserve. For this they would receive a retainer fee which could, incidentally, be used to pay the subscription for the nurse! The Government would then have a readily available fighting force that could be mobilised at any time. Many Uig men over the age of eighteen willingly joined up and received their initial training in Portsmouth. Then from time to time they would have further training, sometimes aboard ships and at other times at the Ross Battery in Steòrnabhagh. Angus Macdonald, Geisiadar, joined the RNR about 1910. He worked at the smelter at Kinlochleven for a time and then moved to a job at Buchanan Street goods station in Glasgow.

On 5th August 1914, the postman delivered buff-coloured envelopes to all the reservists. War had been declared. There was no reluctance to answer the mobilisation call and those on the Island made their way immediately to Steòrnabhagh, thence to Kyle of Lochalsh, and eventually to one of the Channel ports. The most pressing military need at the time was for infantrymen, not for ship's crews, so the Naval Reservists found themselves issued with a rifle and ten rounds of ammunition. Their training had been as crew for warships and the handling of big naval guns, not as infantrymen! However, on 5th October they were transported to Antwerp in Belgium, via Dunkirk, to attempt to defend the strategic port from the advance of the Kaiser's Army. The defences were built in the nineteenth century or before and were no match for heavy artillery or the devastating fire from the 'Big Bertha' mortars. The ill-equipped and inadequately trained Naval Brigades had no chance and held out for less than three days. This tiny force of raw recruits and reservists, were contemptuously nicknamed by the Kaiser, 'Winston's Little Army'. Churchill was First Lord of the Admiralty at the time and having exhorted the Belgians to hold Antwerp at all costs, the only troops he had available to send in support were these RNR sailors. Before they left on the ill-fated expedition Churchill had inspected them, and remarked on what a fine body of men they were. He obviously realised how unprepared they were for the ensuing ordeal.

They were facing overwhelming odds and, despite orders that they were to defend this strategic deepwater port at all costs, it was obvious that a retreat was necessary. There were also specific orders that on no account should the Naval Division be caught in Antwerp. Eventually the orders came to fall back and two of the Brigades did so but for some hours the third remained ignorant of the withdrawal. 3,500 men reached Burght, crossed the River Scheldt by pontoon bridge and marched to St.Niklaas, where they boarded trains and escaped. The other 1,500 men of the 1st Brigade consisting of Hawke, Benbow and Collingwood Battalions finally got their evacuation orders but when they arrived at the river the bridge was no longer in place. Fortunately there were some small boats available for ferrying them across but valuable time had been lost. They arrived exhausted at St.Nicklaas early in the morning of 9th October. All the transport had departed and they were forced to continue on foot to St. Gillis-Waas. There they discovered that the railway had been blown up, and they were almost completely surrounded by enemy troops. In fact some of the Naval Brigade had already been captured, including John Maclean, Ungesiadar, John Buchanan, Breanais, John and Angus Maciver Cradhlastadh, and Donald Mackay Bhaltos. Only three of the Uigeachs who were sent to Antwerp managed to escape that day; they were Kenneth Maciver Geishiadar, Donald Macritchie An Aird and Angus Mackay Bhaltos. The rest were now facing capture, being wounded or even being killed by the fierce bombardment they were suffering. Commodore Henderson was in charge, and the lives of his men depended on him making the right decision. Reluctantly he chose the safest option; rather than becoming prisoners of war, they would cross the border. Once they were on Dutch soil, and had surrendered their weapons to the Dutch Army, they became internees in the neutral country of Holland.

The First Naval Brigade had been fighting for four days, mostly on the retreat, but now their war was over. However, morale was fairly high because at this stage of the war no one expected it to last more than a few months – they would surely be home for Christmas.

HMS Timbertown

Most of the First Royal Naval Brigade found themselves in neutral Holland on 9th October 1914. They were exhausted and filthy. They had not slept or eaten properly for days. Instead they had marched many miles, some of them without their boots because their feet were so swollen. They had survived extremely fierce bombardment from heavy artillery, with very few casualties. But they could no longer be regarded as a fighting force.

The Uig contingent were: Malcolm and Murdo Buchanan (cousins) Breanais; Angus Morrison Islibhig; Angus Macdonald Geisiadar; Donald Morrison, John William Macleod, Angus Macaulay, and James Morrison Bhaltos; Donald Maclennan Cliobh; Kenneth Nicolson Cradhlastadh and Norman Macritchie An Aird. Out of the twenty Uigeachs who were sent to Antwerp only Kenneth Maciver Geisiader, Donald Macritchie An Aird and Angus Mackay Bhaltos avoided capture or internment.

The forlorn remnant of 'Winston's Little Army' spent their first night in Holland sleeping by the roadside, without any food. They were starving, and some resorted to stripping meat from dead cows that they found in the fields. The next day they were taken under armed guard to Groningen, 40 miles to the west. At first the security was very tight. A rule of neutrality was that 'prisoners' who had sought refuge as a way of avoiding capture by the enemy, should not be permitted to escape or return to active duty. In order to protect its neutral status and avoid occupation itself, the Dutch Government was determined to give no favours to the refugees, so the treatment was generally harsh at first.

They were housed at first, in the Rabenhaupt Barracks in Groningen, which were temporarily vacant.

After three months they were moved into huts especially erected for them, next to the State Prison. This new accommodation soon became known by the inmates as HMS Timbertown. The nickname was derived from the wooden huts and the fact that they housed sailors, not 'infantrymen'. Each hut was fairly large and had a number of stoves but internees complained that in the winter, especially at night, they got very cold. In the summer the ventilation was not adequate and the huts became hot and stuffy. The new camp was on the old parade ground with the barracks perimeter fence on one side and the Sterrobos woods on the other. The Rev. Lamont, writing in the Stornoway Gazette of 25th January 1918, observed that imprisonment behind barbed wire, in the flat and featureless countryside, must have been very hard for Lewismen, used to the hills and the sea.

The food was meagre but just about adequate. Some of the men complained that the only meat they got was horsemeat. It had very little fat and most of the inmates eventually grew accustomed to it. Others complained that the meals were too fatty! Each man received half a loaf of bread a day. It tasted as though it was made from potato peelings and grain husks. Later oatmeal appeared and porridge was taken daily. Eventually it was agreed with the authorities that the internees could do their own catering, as long as they stayed within the permitted budget. Tea was a rare treat and letters home begged for supplies. However things were tight in Uig as well, and tea was just as scarce here – so unfortunately for the internees there was none to spare.

As time went on, negotiations between the Dutch and British Governments led to a slackening of the strict security and somewhat better conditions. Inmates were allowed 'shore leave' for a few hours, which meant that they could go into the town of Groningen. Some of the men had already struck up friendships with local girls through the fence and they went on dates to the local cinema with them. On Sunday afternoons the Englische Kamp had become a sightseeing attraction, and townsfolk came to gawp through the fence at the sailors. The inmates were a novelty and at first many of them felt like monkeys in a zoo. The camp itself was soon to open for two hours on Sunday afternoons so that townspeople could visit. They came to watch football matches, to attend concerts and to provide entertainment themselves. Local musicians, choirs and opera groups performed in the camp. The internees also gave concerts in the town for local people to enjoy.

Astonishingly, by 1916 home leave was being permitted. Ostensibly this was only granted on compassionate or medical grounds. A letter from home to the effect that a 'brother had been killed and the family needed help on the croft', was considered enough. The family doctor generally wrote the letters. One request was granted because it was harvest time and the interned sailor's mother was a widow. Angus *Tobaidh* Macdonald had at least two periods of leave during the four years, each of one month's duration. He dutifully returned each time so that others could have the same privilege in their turn. The rule was that if anyone failed to return from leave, then the privilege would be withdrawn from everyone. Needless to say the feeling of companionship and trust among the men meant that no one broke the rule. It is thought that Malcolm Buchanan of No.11 Breanais also came home on leave. No one else is known to have done so but possibly this is because the event has been forgotten or was just not talked about. There were occasions when internees did not return from leave and in these cases the circumstances were out of their control. Some were killed when the ship taking them across the North Sea was sunk by enemy U-boats, and some became prisoners of war when their transport was intercepted by enemy surface craft.

Heroes Not Cowards

Everyone had predicted that the war would be over by Christmas 1914 but in fact it dragged on for another four years. For the First Naval Brigade, now interned in Holland for the duration, the greatest difficulty was coping with the long hours of inactivity. This was a problem for both the British and the Dutch. There were guards appointed by both sides to prevent any trouble occurring. The Dutch authorities were unable to understand why the men could not be sent home. However the rules of war stated that the internees should not be permitted to take any further part in hostilities. Activities were therefore organised to reduce the boredom. Books and materials were sent out from Britain. Study courses were arranged for the sailors. Angus Macdonald attended First Aid and Navigation courses and he recorded what he learnt in a little notebook. Some of the men studied for exams and were able to sit them in the camp. At least one sailor studied for the Ministry and many got merchant seamen certificates. A number of groups and societies started up such as drama, music and crafts. There was soon a thriving cabaret company that put on regular concerts. The men were permitted to take on work outside the camp. Some worked in coal mines, some in shipyards and others on farms. There was a knitting club and the sailors produced jumpers and socks for themselves and to sell. Others who had the skills already made trinket boxes and other wooden items that they could sell. Some of these were shipped back to Britain, and were sold at Selfridges in London. The money they earned could be used to purchase extra food, essentials and other activities such as trips to town to the cinema or bars. As the war dragged on food became scarce in Holland, and in camp its quality and quantity deteriorated seriously. Rats were caught and eaten. Donald Maclennan was desperately hungry and on one occasion when they were working on a farm he and his companions caught and killed a sheep. So as not to draw attention to themselves by lighting a fire, they decided they would have to eat it raw.

The confined nature of the camp meant that exercise consisted of groups of men walking around in circles. Later compulsory route marches were organised, under armed guard, along the stinking canals. There were also sporting activities organised, such as athletics, cricket and especially football. There were numerous teams in the camp and they played against each other. Later there were matches against local Dutch teams. All the activities outside the camp did sometimes lead to trouble. Internees were allowed to frequent the bars in town, as long as they could afford to. On more than one occasion this led to punch ups. The most frequent causes of such aggravation were encounters with visiting German sailors. (As a neutral country, Holland permitted German ships into their ports). Often the police had to be called in to break up the altercations, and the internees would be escorted back to the camp.

It wasn't just visiting sailors who created opportunities for punch ups. The local young men were becoming very jealous because the British 'war-heroes' enchanted the Groningen girls. These men sometimes lay in wait for the sailors, and fights occurred just outside the camp. The fathers and older brothers of the Groningen girls ordered them not to go anywhere near the camp, but this had no effect. It was not long before romances started and there were a number of marriages between the British men and Dutch girls. There was an added advantage to this because a married internee was permitted to spend each night at the home of his wife. However these visits had to be accompanied by a guard who also stayed at the house. Inevitably there were also a number of children born out of wedlock. There are still people in Holland who are trying to discover who their British fathers were.

There were not many escapes, and the British Government discouraged such attempts. In fact one escapee got to the British Consulate and was turned away because they did not want to be seen to be aiding and abetting such behaviour. Those that did manage to get back home did so with the help of the Dutch people who were, on the whole, sympathetic. However in the north of Holland there were some residents who reported suspects to the authorities. One successful escapee arrived home to a very hostile reception from his family. They were concerned that he would be sent into battle again, but that the next time he might not be so lucky.

Time wore on and at last the war came to an end. After four long years the Armistice was signed and the internees could finally go home for good. But would they be greeted as heroes? They had survived a war that had killed 57 out of the 312 Uigeachs who went to fight for King and Country. They had in fact returned fairly unscathed or damaged by their experiences. Angus Macdonald was lucky to avoid a fateful trip back home on the 31st December. Along with other sailors who had survived the war, he arrived by train at Kyle of Lochalsh. He queued patiently on the quayside waiting to board the HMY *Iolaire* but was turned away due to that boat being overcrowded. The boat sailed with far more on board than it was designed for. Angus and the others who could not sail that evening were extremely disappointed. However, it turned out that they were extremely lucky, because most of those on the Iolaire were drowned near Steòrnabhagh harbour, when the boat hit the rocks known as the Beasts of Holm.

Despite being sarcastically accused of 'sleeping in Holland for four years', they were not cowards. They may have had doubts themselves, about whether they had done their bit. They possibly felt that surrendering to a neutral country would not be seen as a very brave thing to do. I found that those who had known these men had little information for me, due to the reticence of the internees to speak about their experiences. These relatives wondered whether the reluctance to talk might have had something to do with embarrassment about the whole thing.

Some of the surviving ex-internees, four of them from Uig, met in Steòrnabhagh for a reunion in October 1959. They had all been in the same hut as Donald Macleod, a Lochsman, who had emigrated to Canada soon after the end of the First War. He later moved to California where he lived for some years, before returning home in 1958. He had quite a bit of money saved and decided that he wanted to meet up with his Groningen friends again. So it was he who arranged and paid for a dinner at the Caledonian Hotel, for the surviving members of his hut. Some of the internees even travelled to Groningen in the same year. These events would have given them an opportunity to reminisce about their shared experiences, without others overhearing them. Unfortunately for us too little of the story of their time in Holland has survived, and they cannot be interviewed now as they are all long dead.

The action that the Commanding Officer took on 9th October 1914 would be judged by today's standards as the only sensible option available to him. However the standards of that time did call into question the decision. The men of the First Naval Brigade had all enthusiastically answered the call of their country, without question. Each and every man would willingly have given his life, had the circumstances at the fall of Antwerp, not conspired to save rather than sacrifice them. In fact it must have taken great courage for a trained sailor to face the onslaught of a well-prepared invading army, with only a rifle and ten rounds of ammunition to fight with! They were in fact heroes, who just happened to cheat death, and survive the war!

ACKNOWLEDGEMENTS

As I was not present at any of the events or incidents described in my articles, I often felt the need to research further and speak to others, just to get additional perspectives on topics Iain and I discussed. I felt I was writing articles to be read, not just in Uig but also in distant parts of the world, so including other people's information would be useful.

I am grateful therefore, not only to Iain *Tobaidh* who provided the vast majority of the stories, but must also thank the following people, who contributed in one way or another to the articles.

David Fowler of Steòrnabhagh Library, Mark Elliott of Museum nan Eilean, and in no particular order; Ina Macdonald, Calum Buchanan, Donald Maciver, Annie Macleod, Alison Bremner, Dolol and Peggy Ann Macdonald, Murdina Maclennan, Norman Macdonald, Finn Morrison, Iain Buchanan, Joni Buchanan, D.J.Macleod, Mary Ann Buchanan, Finlay Maciver, Agnes Bethune, Katy Mary Macleod, Guido Blokland, Menno Welinga, John Murdo Maclean, Teen Ann Murray, Norman Macaulay, Alexander Smith, Pat Macfarlane, Rodney Long and David Hanson. The archives at Comunn Eachdraidh Uig and The Stornoway Gazette.

To Catriona Nicholson, Lynda Edwardes-Evans and Donna Macdonald for providing editorial support and Alasdair Macdonald and Chris Macdonald in helping make this book a reality.

If I have missed out anyone from this list, I am very sorry for the omission.

Uig, Isle of Lewis

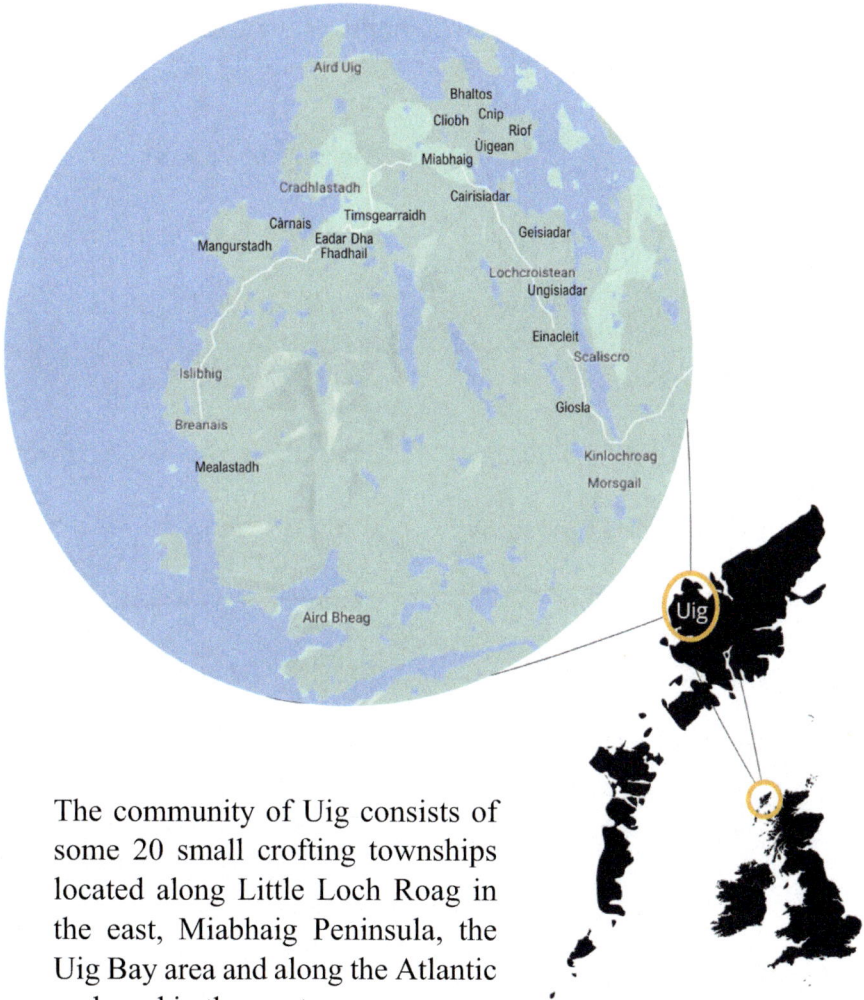

The community of Uig consists of some 20 small crofting townships located along Little Loch Roag in the east, Miabhaig Peninsula, the Uig Bay area and along the Atlantic seaboard in the west.

Text courtesy of Comunn Eachdraidh Uig
http://www.ceuig.co.uk/places/villages
Uig Map: Google Maps

Bailtean Uig

Na Bailtean / The Villages of Uig are listed in Gaelic and English in order from the beginning of the Uig road to the end at Mealastadh.

Giosla / Gisla

Einacleit / Enaclete

Ungisiadar / Ungeshader

Lochcroistean

Geisiadar / Geshader

Cairisiadar / Carishader

Miabhaig / Maivaig

Cliobh / Cliff

Bhaltos / Valtos

Cnìp / Kneep

Riof / Reef

Ùigean / Uigen

Eireastadh / Erista

Àird Ùig / Aird Uig

Cradhlastadh / Crowlista

Timsgearraidh / Timsgarry

Eadar Dha Fhadhail / Ardroil

Càrnais / Carnish

Mangurstadh / Mangersta

Ìslibhig / Islivig

Breanais / Breanish

Mealastadh / Mealista

About The Author

David Roberts taught in primary schools in Yorkshire for almost 20 years and holidayed in the Isle of Lewis every summer with his wife Rosie and daughter Alice. He took early retirement when the tenancy of a croft in the Uig district became available and moved to Islibhig in 1991. David's interests include geology, wildlife, archaeology and local history. He is a Trustee of Comunn Eachdraidh Uig, and served on the committee as secretary and chairperson for over 12 years. He continues to have an avid interest in local history, and supports the museum, including providing primary school children with an experience of Viking life, through drama and practical activities.

It was David's great privilege to hear Iain Tobaidh's memories of life in the beautiful Outer Hebrides and be encouraged to retell them in print for the enjoyment of a wider audience.

Printed in Great Britain
by Amazon